Paint Your House
like a Pro

Paint Your House like a Pro

Tips from A to Z on
Painting Your House Inside and Out

by **Will Charnow**

The
Globe
Pequot
Press

Chester, Connecticut

Interior artwork courtesy Glidden/ICI Paints
Interior photography courtesy Kevin Edwards

Library of Congress Cataloging-in-Publication Data

Charnow, Will.
    Paint your house like a pro: tips from A to Z on painting your house inside and out/
Will Charnow
        p.   cm.
    ISBN 0-87106-306-9
    1. House painting. I. Title.
    TT320.C48 1991
    698'.1—dc20
                                                                        90-24251
                                                                        CIP

Manufactured in the United States of America
First Globe Pequot Edition/First Printing

Contents

Contents

Contents

Contents

Preface

In the early 1970s, I got a job at a large paint store as a delivery driver. During my months of working for the store, I would look at all the different paint can labels and try to understand them, but they might as well have been written in Chinese. I saw painting contractors all the time and said to myself, "I'll never become a painter; it's too messy, and the fumes are horrendous."

Well, I needed to make more money and there was no room for advancement in the company at the time, so I got another job—with a professional painter who had been painting custom homes for thirty years. I worked for him for a year, and it was hard work, to say the least. A perfectionist, he never took a break during the day except for a half-hour lunch. While working for him, however, I got to do a little of everything, the result being I learned a lot and became adept at painting.

After doing some small painting jobs by myself, I went to work for another painting contractor with thirty-some years of experience. During my year with him, I added considerably to my knowledge and abilities. Then I worked for yet another contractor, and another, and another—and still another. Finally, in 1976, I started my own business. It is still going strong.

My seventeen years in the business have enabled me to find the fastest and best ways to prep, patch, undercoat, and finish-coat just about anything except NASA rockets. Sure, I made mistakes, but that's just the point: Because I did, you don't have to. This book presents each and every one of those best and fastest ways, learned on my own and by working with several veteran contractors and interviewing hundreds more, along with many a store manager. I am confident as a result that this book provides the best, most up-to-date information on how to do quality, fast painting that lasts a long time and looks great. I hope, after following my suggestions on your next project, that you will agree.

Happy painting.

Do the Job Right

I've organized this guide from A to Z to help you zero in on the information you need quickly and easily. If you are undertaking a big job for the first time, however, consult the following entries for interiors or exteriors in the order given, along with the accompanying equipment lists. They indicate the proper order of steps—and the proper materials—needed for doing the job right the first time.

EXTERIORS

Preparation

Specific Surfaces
(refer to the appropriate entries)

Painting Tips and Techniques

Equipment—Exteriors

Required

Optional

INTERIORS

Preparation

Enamels (undercoater), Masonry condi-tioner, Metals (conditioner), Rust (rust-resistant primer), Sanding sealer, Shellac, Stain-killer sealer, Surface bonder

Specific Surfaces
(refer to the appropriate entries)

Painting Tips and Techniques

Equipment—Interiors

Required

Optional

Paint Your House
like a Pro

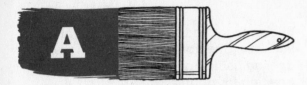

Accent colors are tones that stand out to contrast in color or intensity with a neutral ground or surrounding surface. They can be factory-prepared or custom-mixed at your paint store. **Accent paints** are factory-made, solid, pure, colors, such as black, yellow, blue, and red and are usually used on surfaces for dramatic effect. *See* **Fluorescent colors, Paints.**

Acetone is a colorless, volatile, extremely flammable liquid that is used as an organic mixing solvent and as a cleaner on some surfaces, such as concrete. Acetone will attack many paint films and is toxic.

Acids can be used to clean and prepare metal and concrete surfaces for painting. Use caution and protect your skin and eyes when working with acids, and stay away from their fumes. When diluting acids, never add water to acid because the water will boil and splatter onto your face or body; instead add acid to water slowly, stirring constantly. Acid solutions should be mixed in plastic or glass containers. *See* **Etching, Hydrochloric acid, Muriatic acid, Phosphoric acid,** and **Health and safety.**

Acoustic ceilings can be composed of sound-absorption panels that hang from a metal grid, or they can be made of a light, textured material applied directly to the ceiling and referred to in the trade as "popcorn," "oatmeal," or "cottage cheese."

This material can be applied in a number of ways. It can come premixed in a tub or as a roll-on patching mixture. It can be sprayed on with a portable texture gun. There are also specially made acoustic-spray rigs that are used to apply most of the new acoustic ceilings; they can also be used for retexturing older acoustic ceilings or for patching. These machines are expensive, but they produce the best texture. For best results, whichever method you use, be sure to cover the surface with several passes.

Some painting companies specialize in spraying and repairing acoustic ceilings. Consult the yellow pages for one of these companies if you don't have the necessary experience and equipment to do it yourself. Even if you are a budding professional, it might pay to subcontract this part of the job until you feel comfortable with what you are doing.

Newly blown acoustic ceilings require a straight, even line, or bead line, where ceiling and walls meet. Move a straight-edge or stick of some sort along the ceiling and wall meeting line to scrape off enough acoustic material to leave a nice straight line. Without a bead line, the edges of the ceiling will look ragged when the walls are painted.

Quick patches, stucco patch, plaster of paris, and spackle can all be used to fill cracks and holes in acoustic ceilings, prior to texturing with matching acoustic patching materials. Use a shellac primer or a quick-drying stain-killer sealer on completely dried-out water-damaged areas to prevent them from later bleeding through finish-paint coats.

Before painting, vacuum the ceiling so that it's free from dust, lint, cobwebs, and loose particles. Acoustic ceilings that are dirty or stained can be cleaned with a strong solution of T.S.P. (trisodium phosphate) and water, sprayed with a garden pump-action sprayer. Rinse the treated areas on the ceiling with clean water afterward.

There are specially made acoustic-ceiling paints. However, most good-quality flat paints may be used. Acoustic ceilings are typically top-coated with interior white or off-white flat water-based finish paints, rather than with enamel paints.

The best way to repaint acoustic ceilings is with an airless sprayer. *See* **Spraying.** Spray an acoustic ceiling lengthwise in one pass and then across in one pass for the best results. A thin coat of paint is recommended, or the work will look globby. A thick coat on a perforated tile ceiling will mean you'll spend most of your time pricking open painted-over holes, using toothpicks.

Glitter may be applied to acoustic ceilings by mixing it into the paint solution before it is sprayed on, or by shooting it on after the ceiling has been painted.

There are specially made acoustic-ceiling roller covers. Rolling or brushing out acoustic ceilings is not recommended in most cases, however, because it is neck- and backbreaking work and takes a long time to do. *See also* **Ceilings, Prep work,** and **Spraying.**

Acrylic is a man-made plasticlike resin used in the manufacture of many water-based paints. Paints that are 100 percent acrylic have a very good reputation; the enamels are excellent, and the flat paints are the most durable of all flat paints. Some acrylic paints are made with latex or vinyl resins to create a vinyl-acrylic or latex-acrylic paint. Most of the best water-based exterior and masonry paints are made with acrylic resins. Acrylic coatings have great color-holding qualities and are a good alternative to oil-based (or alkyd-resin) paints. *See also* **Paint.**

Most water-based paints can be ruined if the can is stored in the cold. Also, check the label to determine the coldest temperature at which the paint can be applied.

Adhesion: For a good painting job, the paints must adhere, or bond, to the surface. Most paint labels will tell you the types of surfaces that the paint is designed for and to paint only clean, dry surfaces, free from loose particles and peeling paint. Follow the label, or you're heading for trouble.

Plaster glue helps some patching materials stick better to surfaces. *See also* **Cleaning, Glue, Prep work,** and **Surface-bonder.**

Airless sprayer: *See* **Spraying.**

Alkali is a powdery substance that can form on masonry surfaces, such as brick and concrete. It is caustic and can eat through paint coats that are applied over it. The lime used in many plasters is an alkali. Treat an alkali surface with a mild acid, like vinegar, before painting. *See also* **Efflorescence** and **Masonry.**

Alkyd is a man-made resin used in the making of many oil-based paints. There are some cheaper, water-based vinyl-alkyd paints on the market, but these are not recommended for best results. Some of the best premium oil-based enamels are made from alkyd resins. If you want to use an oil-based enamel paint that is less prone to leaving lap marks, bonds well, and keeps its gloss for a long time, then consider using oil-based alkyd enamel paints.

Many synthetic resins are temperature-sensitive and cannot be used on cold days; check the label. *See also* **Paint.**

Aluminum surfaces must be cleaned and scratched before applying paint. It is a good idea to use steel wool on a new aluminum surface to help achieve a better bond. Or, if possible, let new aluminum weather for six weeks or longer before painting it. *See* **Etching.**

For outdoor applications, make sure your paint or undercoat is suited for aluminum. Interior aluminum surfaces not exposed to sunlight or water, however, can be painted over with almost any finish paint.

Aluminum paints, sometimes called "silver" paint, can be made by using aluminum dust or aluminum flakes. Paint made from flakes is better because the flakes overlap to form a more solid film. Aluminum paint makes a good sealant when applied over spots that can bleed through. Bear in mind, though, that the aluminum color may be hard to cover with light-colored paints. Aluminum paints are great for marine environments, because they resist moisture. As a roof coating, aluminum paints work well because they reflect heat. Most mobile-home roofs are made of aluminum.

Always stir an aluminum paint well. When using aluminum spray paint, shake the can often.

Ambidextrous: For a full-time painter, being "one-handed" is a real liability. Two hands work faster than one. When up on a ladder, being ambidextrous is advantageous because you don't have to stop and move the ladder so frequently, and it is safer because you aren't awkwardly reaching as often. Working with both hands is also easier on your body.

Most people are ambidextrous to some extent; you may be able to type, for instance, exhibiting equal use of both hands. You lose the ability to use both hands equally when you constantly favor one over the other. To become ambidextrous, start using your opposite hand for some activities. It will take some time for your "wrong" hand to catch up and become comfortable, but persist, and you'll be glad you did.

Ammonia is a good grease remover and the best cleaner for smoke accumulation. It can also be used decoratively to darken some woods, such as oak.

Ammonia is a strong cleaner and should be used with caution. Test a small part of your surface first to see if gloss or the like will be affected. As a general rule,

work quickly and rinse as soon as possible. Never mix different kinds of cleansers. Bleach and ammonia, for instance, form a poisonous gas.

Antiques may be paintings, statues, carpets, furniture, servingware or trinkets. They are expensive and often cannot be replaced. What might be considered normal clean-up or minor work damage to an ordinary object may be a disaster if the object is an antique. Antiques should be covered well with drop cloths or plastic sheeting. Better yet, they should be removed from the painting area. The bottom line is: Be careful when working around any household goods, especially antiques.

Antiquing is making an object appear to be aged. Antiquing a surface can be achieved by using an acrylic enamel, followed after thorough drying by an oil-based semi-transparent stain. There are good books that deal specifically with antiquing and graining. Ask a paint dealer for his antiquing brochures or already finished samples of antiquing on wood. Consider antiquing the front doors of a building for an especially elegant look. *See also* **Graining.**

Appearances: If you are a full-time painter, it is a good idea to look neat and to wear "painting whites" (bib overalls) or white pants with a white tee-shirt or short-sleeved shirt. This way, you will be regarded as a professional and you'll inspire confidence in your customers, paint dealers, boss, or employees. This is especially important if you are just learning the basics, or you haven't yet achieved a solid reputation.

Your work vehicle, whether it is a truck, van, station wagon or car, should be as clean as possible. White or off-white vehicles are usually associated with painters and painting, but a clean van or truck of any color is impressive.

Your work area should be neat, orderly and covered at night. Work with drop cloths always whenever you prep, patch or paint. Professionalism pays.

Apprentices: In the painting union's apprentice programs, it takes up to four years before a person is considered a journeyman, or professional, painter. In the non-union painting shops, a person's past work determines his status as a journeyman painter. A professional painter earns two to five times as much as an apprentice painter.

If you are an apprentice painter, aim to become a journeyman as directly as possible. This will involve study, concentration, increasing responsibility, and always pushing to become faster at doing quality work. There's a lot of satisfaction in painting. You will be surprised at how your pride grows as you become professional, make more money, and earn the respect of others.

Attitude is important because it affects the outcome of your work. If you are uptight, depressed, burned out or just tired of working, chances are you'll make mistakes, forget to do something or take forever to get a job done. If your attitude is generally positive, you will be able to cruise through the work. Things will seem easier, even on a difficult job.

It's especially important to maintain a positive attitude if you're a professional painter. Customers will find less fault with your work and give you fewer problems. Even if your customers are negative or real picky about your work, don't take it personally; simply go on with the job, and do the same old good work you always do. The job will turn out nice, and you consequently should get paid on time.

Automatic paint shakers: Most paint dealers have shakers that hold one to four cans of paint at a time. They shake paint vigorously from one to ten minutes, depending on how the timer is set.

It is always a good idea to have paint shaken when you buy it. This includes stock and custom-colored paints, as well as primers, sealers, undercoaters and stains. Also, if you buy paint in bulk, a good paint dealer should reshake a can for you when you want to use it. However, never have clear coating finishes, such as varnish or lacquer, shaken. It causes thousands of bubbles.

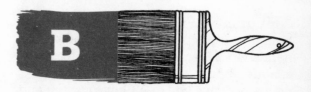

Back-priming is the painting of the back side of objects that are to be placed flush against a wall or other surface. Sometimes baseboards, shutters, and trim work are back-primed before they are set in place. Back-priming seals the surface and gives you some protection against cracking and warping. When back-priming, be careful not to drip over onto the other side of the object.

Baked finish is a paint finish done in a specially designed oven room with infrared lights. Commercial and industrial businesses most often use baked finishes. If a baked finish is under consideration, make sure the surface to be painted can tolerate high heat.

Baseboards: The recommended finish paint for baseboards is enamel, because it looks better, is more durable, and is easier to clean than flat paint. Baseboards are usually painted last.

On new baseboards, a three-coat paint system is recommended for durability, but an undercoater topped with a finish coat is often acceptable. The undercoat can be applied anytime, but don't apply any finish coats until all other painting has been done and the baseboards are free of drips and splatters.

When painting ceilings and walls, it is a good idea to cover the baseboards to prevent roller spray and drips from getting on them. When rolling above a baseboard, keep your drop cloths over the baseboards to protect them. Check your drop cloths from time to time, to make sure they haven't slipped. Masking tape or a paint shield blade can keep paint off a floor or carpet when you are painting a baseboard.

When painting finish coats on baseboards, it is a good idea to pour only an inch or two of the finish paint in a 1-gallon can or bucket and use it only on baseboards. This way, dust and dirt will not contaminate your whole supply of paint. For the same reason, throw away any unused portion of this baseboard paint that is left after finishing all the baseboards, rather than pouring it back into the can.

Basements are typically damp. Depending on the surface you are painting (walls, floor, or ceiling), make sure you use the right undercoater before putting on a finish coat. If the basement walls are prone to efflorescence (the formation of powdery deposits), a surface-bonder mixed in with the first coat of paint may be needed. Treat any mildew with a bleach solution to remove it before painting. A stain killer or a shellac primer may be needed on scuff marks, water-damaged areas that have completely dried out, or other bleed-through problems that have been prepped or patched up. For finish coats consider using a moisture-proof paint that says so on its label, a rubber-based paint, an industrial enamel, or a specifically labeled basement paint for best results.

There are thick masonry waterproofing paints that can be used on bare cement or masonry walls to alleviate water leaks and wet-wall problems. These paints can best be applied by using stiff-bristled brushes. A fan and dehumidifier can aid in helping basement walls to dry faster.

Consider using a dehumidifier and/or sump pump full-time in problem basements. *See also* **Paints, Masonry, Mildew, Stain-killer sealer,** and **Surface bonder.**

Bathroom: To prepare a bathroom for painting, lay drop cloths on the floor. Then cover the sink, shower, and bathtub areas with cloth or plastic drops. Next, remove any hardware you think will be in the way. Keep the screws and parts together and label or code the parts. Put all the hardware in a place where it won't get painted or disturbed. Any grease, grime, oils, dirt, or tobacco stains should be cleaned with a T.S.P. (trisodium phosphate) solution and then rinsed clean with clear water. Next, break the gloss on any ceilings and walls that are glossy, using a sanding pole or a liquid deglosser or both. Hand-sand all the trim-work on doors, casings, cabinets, dressers, and the like. Do all the necessary caulking, spackling, and puttying. After everything is completely dry, use the appropriate undercoaters and stain-killer sealers where needed.

I recommend using a semi-gloss or high-gloss alkyd enamel for a bathroom or shower ceiling instead of a water-based enamel. Use a 7-inch roller with a smooth roller cover, and a 2½-inch to 3-inch brush. For larger walls and ceilings use a 9-inch roller and a bigger brush. Do the ceiling first, the walls next, and then the trim work. Paint the baseboards and base trim last. *See also* **Prep work** and **Enamels.**

Bidding: Among the things a bid should include are the length of time the prep work will take; the quantity of prep materials and undercoaters needed; the length of time the undercoaters will take to apply; the quantity of finish paint needed; the number of coats needed; and the length of time it will take to apply the finish paint coats.

After completing your list and figuring out material costs and your hourly rate, add about 10 percent to the bid to cover the unexpected.

Painting bids depend on a given situation. Painters who really need work will usually submit a lower bid than when they are booked solid with work. Sometimes painters will submit a high bid because they really don't want the job, yet they don't want to come out and say so.

A full-time painter should analyze why he got a certain bid, and why he lost another. He should consider the price, his timing and salesmanship, and the client's needs and wants. Many large-volume painting contractors do bidding on jobs based upon a set square footage price. This is done frequently on large commercial jobs.

Bleach, that familiar household liquid, is great for getting rid of mildew and bacteria. Use one part bleach to three or four parts water for mild cases. Use stronger solutions or full-strength bleach for severe and stubborn mildew. Add T.S.P. (trisodium phpsphate) to increase the wetting characteristics. Weathered bare wood that has moisture stains or black or brownish dirty streaks or spots can be cleaned with bleach used at full strength.

Make sure all bleach is completely removed from a surface before painting, otherwise the bleach can spot and bleed through the finish coats applied over it. When using bleach, avoid getting it on trees, bushes, plants, thresholds or on any natural finishes. Avoid contact with your skin, and for safety, it is a good idea to wear safety goggles to protect your eyes.

Bleaching wood is usually done to create a bare blondish-white, or off-white appearance. Household bleach mixed with water or used straight can be used for bleaching some woods. Also, there are more powerful commercial wood bleaches, usually made with oxalic acid and ready for use after mixing with water. Caution: Oxalic acid is highly toxic. Avoid ingesting or inhaling fumes, and contact with the skin. It's a good idea to wear rubber gloves when using commercial wood bleaches.

Before bleaching an entire area or surface it is a good idea to experiment in a small, unnoticeable spot. Apply a clear finish or semi-transparent stain over the rinsed and dried bleached area to see if it's what you really want before bleaching an entire area.

A streaky or uneven semi-transparent stain job can usually be fixed by bleaching, followed by the correct application of a semi-transparent stain.

Finishes for bleached surfaces include a semi-transparent stain only, or a semi-transparent stain and a clear finish, or a clear finish only.

Bleeding or **bleed-through** is a term used to describe just about anything that comes through a finish coat of paint.

Rust spots must be chipped, sanded, cleaned, and then spot-primed with a rust-resistant primer, otherwise they will bleed through. Allow the primer to dry thoroughly before applying a finish coat. Sometimes a fast-drying stain-killer sealer must be applied over the rust-resistant primer, when a white or off-white color is the finish paint, to prevent the deeply colored red of the primer from bleeding through.

Knots, stains, and spots in wood should be first cleaned and spot-primed with an appropriate shellac primer or stain-killer sealer, otherwise they may bleed through enamels, flat paints, or other similar kinds of finish pigmented paints. Many different kinds of bare wood will bleed through enamels and flat paints if a wood undercoater is not applied first. Surfaces with dark or deep colors in a flat or enamel finish should be sealed over with a stain-killer sealer if a white or light color is to go on over them; otherwise, they can bleed through. Some water-based undercoaters will not stop certain things like sap, oily scuff marks, and smoke damage from bleeding through, so an oil-based stain-killer sealer sometimes must be applied.

Most oil-based sealers and stain killers are more effective than water-based sealers, but don't use oil-based products directly on bare drywall, because the paper surface will "nap up."

Bare, unpainted cedar and redwood are prone to bleeding through, so a strong oil-based undercoater or a stain-killer sealer should be applied when an enamel or pigmented flat paint are to be the finish coats.

Stains caused by resins from knots in bare wood should be treated as follows: If the stain cleans up with water, use an oil-based paint as the final coat. If the stain cleans up with mineral spirits or a similar solvent, use a water-based finish paint as the final coat. Smoke streaks, scuff marks, and water-damaged areas that have already dried and been prepped should be spot-sealed with a stain-killer sealer or a shellac primer. Otherwise they can bleed through finish paint coats that are applied directly over them. *See* **Prep work.**

Blisters: Most blistering results from a water problem or excess moisture. Water somehow got behind the paint film and eventually caused it to separate from the surface, which created blisters, also called bubbles. Green or wet wood can cause blistering. Undried patching materials, or improperly sealed patches can cause blistering. Failure to let an undercoater or first finish coat dry completely can cause subsequent coats of paint to blister. There are other causes of blistering: Paint applied over bare metal lacking an undercoater can bubble. Cheap or overly thinned paints may blister, especially when they are applied over smooth or glossy surfaces. Even quality premium paints can blister if they're applied to a hot, sun-baked surface.

When trouble-shooting a blistering problem, look for moisture first. Remove all loose paint and reprep the area, making sure the surface is sealed for good adhesion. The solution to most blistering problems is proper prep work. *See* **Prep work.**

Block walls (made with concrete, plaster, or brick and mortar) should be painted just like most other masonry or stucco surfaces. Very porous block walls, however, can be treated the same way as cinder-block walls and fences. Cinder blocks are porous concrete with large, hollow cavities. They are usually made of slag or cinder, cement, and sand, whereas most concrete walls are made of sand, gravel, and cement.

Unpainted cinder blocks require a minimum of two coats of paint, but additional coats are recommended for better results. On prepainted cinder blocks or block walls, efflorescence must be removed first if it is present. On chalky cinder block or block-wall surfaces, after cleaning and scraping is done, a clear surface bonder added to the first coat of paint is recommended before finish coats are applied.

Water-based masonry paints are highly recommended as finish coats on cinder block.

Spraying cinder or block walls with an airless sprayer, followed by a person using a roller to work the wet paint into the pores, is the fastest method. Use a 1-

inch or 1¼-inch roller cover when rolling out cinder or block walls, and firmly work the roller cover into all the holes and crevices. It could take a month of Sundays to thoroughly paint a cinder or block wall by brushing only. You can first apply a block filler to a cinder or block wall if a smoother surface is desired. *See also* **Concrete, Masonry,** and **Paint.**

Blow torch: Heat aids the removal of paint. A blow torch, usually propane, or an electric heat-scraper, or an infra-red lamp can be used to remove paint. Train the torch at an angle, about ¾-inch to 1½ inches away from the painted surface. Follow about 3 or 4 inches behind the torched area with a scraper. As soon as the paint begins to bubble, scrape it off.

Most heat removal is done on exterior surfaces. For interior surfaces, a chemical paint remover is recommended. Even on exterior surfaces, regard blow-torching as a last resort. Burning paint off is dangerous and tedious. Resinous woods and other flammables present a real fire hazard. Yet sometimes, it is the only way to get old paint off completely. Proceed very carefully, checking frequently all around where you're working to make sure heat isn't building into a flame. Don't burn paint off on windy days. Check your gas lines for leaks. Wear a particle mask, cloth gloves and safety glasses. *See also* **Paint removers.**

Blushing refers to a whitening effect that occurs on a surface, which can usually be traced to a moisture problem. Also, too much thinning of a paint can sometimes result in blushing.

Boats are subjected to extremely adverse conditions for paint. For best results use only specially formulated marine-type paints and materials on boats.

Body: Paints that cover well are said to have "body" (more pigments and resins). Body therefore is proportional to the amount of solids and overall thickness of a paint. A stain that has a solid look to it and covers well over surfaces is called a solid-body stain.

Bonder: Anything that is applied before a coat of paint or patching material, or that's added to it to increase adhesion may be called a bonder. A plaster and cement glue, or a regular old white household glue (which you add yourself, with a light hand) when used in cement or stucco-patching mixes are bonders, and good ones, at that, for making these mixes adhere better to a surface. *See* **Surface bonder.**

Boxing of paints is a slang term for mixing all the same kind and color together before you start painting with them. Boxing guarantees a uniform color, consistency, and sheen. Flats, enamels, undercoaters, primers, sealers, and stains can all be boxed in this way: First, lay down a drop cloth. Open all the cans of paint and put the lids away from where you will be boxing. Take two or more clean, empty, and dry cans and put them next to the full cans. Next, pour the correct amount of thinning agent in the empty cans, so that as you box the paint, you thin at the same time. Now start pouring the full cans—a little bit at a time—into the empty cans. Move in a circular fashion, going back and forth like musical chairs, pouring one can into another, filling three or four up and having one or two less than full. Repeat this cycle about five or six times, until you have uniformly mixed cans of paint, each with the same color and consistency.

Pouring paint is important and deserves a few words: When you are through pouring a full 5-gallon can into another "five," hit the lip of the 5-gallon container you're pouring into with your empty can at a downward angle, overlapping the full can by a couple of inches, quickly pull away, bringing the can you're pouring from right-side up. This will prevent drips and spills.

Don't shake or box clear finishes; it introduces bubbles. Instead stir these finishes with a light hand.

Until you become skillful and accurate, use at least two extra containers for boxing or mixing any paints or undercoaters. Pigments and other solids that are stuck to the bottom or sides of a paint can must be mixed completely with the rest of the paint; this can't usually be done by stirring only. Consider putting 95 percent of the paint into a larger can or bucket. Then scrape the sticky pigments from the original paint can into the other can. Stir.

Any paint or undercoater that doesn't respond to mixing, shaking, or boxing may be a bad batch, or might have been sitting around in the store too long. Consider returning the paint or throwing it away.

It is a good idea to stir from time to time any paints you are using, while painting, to maintain uniform consistency.

Stir paints with paint-store stir sticks, using a circular motion. Try to bring the bottom material to the top of the surface as you are stirring. Always stir paints before using them, until there are no thinning agents floating on the top of the paint.

Brass: In almost all cases brass should not be painted. However, if brass is to be painted, find the strongest metal undercoater and prime it first. Then apply a finish coat, using an industrial or epoxy enamel paint for best durability.

Brick should be treated like any other masonry surface for undercoating and finish coating. Wire brushes, scrapers, putty knives, and electric sanders are used to prepare brick that has previously been painted.

For best results, new brick should age at least 12½ to 15½ months before painting. *See also* **Efflorescence, Fireplaces, Masonry,** and **Paint.**

A **Broad-knife** is a 4-to-6-inch-wide putty knife used for applying spackle, joint compound, and other patching materials. Patching is usually done in several passes, always aiming toward a smoother surface. The finer the surface, the larger the knife you'll want to use.

Broad-knives are also handy for opening stuck windows and doors and for scraping, chipping, and cleaning out cracks.

Always carry a broad-knife on any painting job. It is a good idea to buy better quality and more expensive broad-knives. In the long run, a quality broad-knife will be worth its price in durability and strength.

Broken areas: Perhaps the only time you'll see the words, "broken areas," is in a painting contract that spells out everything in detail. Broken areas are places that need prep work, such as chipping, sanding, or patching.

Broom: Brooms are handy and can be used for sweeping overhangs, getting rid of cobwebs from ceilings and corners, and meeting other needs that arise from time to time. There is always some clean up or sweeping that needs to be done on painting projects.

Brushes: A cheap brush can never produce as good a custom finish as a good-quality brush. Use the best brushes for the best work.

A good-quality paint brush holds paint

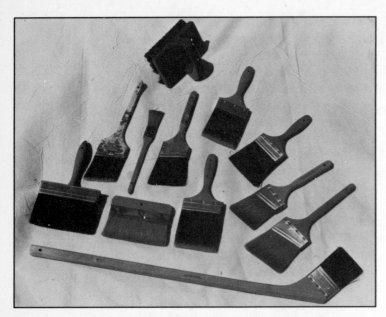

Brushes come in all sizes and shapes. The back brush is called a rough-rider (for staining). Second brush in the front is a duster brush (for dusting purposes only). The two brushes in the front right are called sash, or angular, brushes (they are especially good for painting windows). The long, angled brush in the front is called a hockey-stick.

well, doesn't drip much, and shouldn't leave noticeable brush marks. Quality brushes cost more, but they are well worth it. The bristles on a good brush taper, being thicker at the base than at the tips. This gives them proper flexibility, allowing them to bend more at the tips than at the base, for sensitive action. Each bristle also divides at the tip to form tiny branches, or "flags," that hold more paint. The bristles are gathered in the ferrule at various lengths, which gives the brush better flow and leveling capabilities. When you press a quality brush against your hand, it should feel thick, not hollow. It should feel solid and lively, with good spring. Quality brushes work better, faster, and give more paint coverage than cheap brushes. They're also easier to clean and last longer.

Cheap brushes are not hand-made and usually have plastic handles instead of wooden ones. The bristles are of an even thickness and length, not good for holding or applying paint. The overall shape is awkward, often too short for the width, and the feel is either too stiff or too soft. The ferrules are loose and in a short time the bristles begin to fall out.

Foam brushes and kalsomine brushes are not recommended for fine-quality painting.

China bristles (actually hog hair) make the best brushes for painting with oil-based paints. China bristles can be black, brown, or white. The price will determine which one has the better quality when they are made by the same manufacturer. Favor the longer-bristled brushes.

Natural-bristle brushes should never be used with water or water-based paints. They will swell, become limp, fluff out, and not be good for fine work afterwards. Use natural brushes with oil-based paints only.

Nylon, polyester, and tynex brushes can be used with all water-based paints. Synthetic brushes can be used for finish work with oil-based paints, but most painters prefer natural bristles for oil. Synthetic brushes are generally less expensive than bristle brushes, but they can perform very well. When nylon brushes were first introduced, they were pretty clumsy. But now good-quality nylon bristles are very close in character to natural bristles.

Don't use synthetic brushes with lacquers, any paints that require reducers, or hot thinners such as acetone, as they will get ruined. For best results, don't apply varnishes, polyurethanes, shellacs, or enamels with nylon brushes. Badger brushes, which are more expensive, work quite well with varnishes and other clear finishes.

In the old painting days before rollers, 5-inch and 6-inch brushes were used to paint ceilings and walls. Today a 4-inch brush is usually the biggest brush used. However, breaking out a 5-inch or 6-inch brush for some brush work is still done by some painters.

Bare wood or painted wood handles that have been sanded have the best grip.

Always clean a brush thoroughly after use and store it in a keeper, sleeve, or brush holder to keep the bristles together. (*See* **Clean-up.**) Store a brush by hanging it, if possible. Don't store a brush on its tips, as that may ruin it. If necessary, plastic bags or aluminum foil can be used to store an uncleaned paint brush overnight. However, the seal around the brush should be air-tight, and the brush stored in a cool area away from heat.

If you should have to replace or reglue a handle, epoxy works quite well. However, a new brush may be in order at this time.

Brushing alone as a painting method is useful on trim work, furniture, corners, edges, and odd-shaped objects. Brushes are essential for cutting-in around roller work on almost any surface, with almost any paint or undercoater.

It takes time to become good, accurate, and fast with a paint brush, so be patient if you are just starting out. Work on your quality first. Then, work on speeding up. Working faster should not mean working sloppy.

Generally speaking, holding a paint brush near the base of the bristles gives you a more comfortable and better grip. Wall brushes that are 4 inches to 6 inches wide are gripped most of the time using the entire hand, whereas most brushes 3½ inches and smaller, especially sash or angular brushes, are gripped just like a pencil.

When dipping your brush into a paint can, make sure the can is not more than a third or half full with paint. Dip your brush into the container and get paint on it, going no more than halfway up the bristles. Lightly slap the insides of the can or bucket, with both flat wide sides of your brush, then take it out and brush with it. In the painting world this is called the "dip-and-slap" method. Don't wipe the brush off on the sides of the rim of the bucket or can, because you won't have much paint to work with. Every once in a while, how-

The photo above shows the correct grip and technique for painting the sides of a window mullion.

ever, you should wipe the brush horizontally across the paint can or bucket to get out the excess paint in the base of the brush.

A strong wire (as from a clothes hanger) placed across the top of the paint bucket is sometimes useful for fine brushwork when working with clear finishes. After you dip your brush in the paint can, you then smooth the brush along the wire or lightly tap the wire with the brush. Any lint, miscellaneous particles, excess paint, and so forth should end up on the wire or back in the paint, not on your brush or the side of the can. This painting method is usually called either the "wire method" or the "varnishing pot method."

Before using any brush, knock or brush it against the sides of your hand, to get rid of any dust, dirt, or unwanted particles. Always have a drop cloth below anything you are brushing. Always carry

After dipping your brush in paint, gently slap both flat sides of your brush against the inside of the can before brushing paint on a surface. This is called the "dip and slap" method.

a rag when brushing to clean up spills or drips, and also to clean your paint-brush handle when paint drips down on it. Failure to get all the water or thinners out of a cleaned brush could cause dripping down the brush handle and then down your arm. Occasionally wiping your brush horizontally across the paint can or bucket rim you are using will put the excess paint back in the can.

When brushing areas (not cutting-in), as with doors, broad trim, and furniture, lay on (put on) the paint west to east or vice-versa, then lay off (brush out) north to south or vice-versa. Generally speaking, you lay on the shortest part of the surface, and you lay off along the longest distance.

Always brush into or lay off towards your last wet edge. Don't brush too far ahead with enamels or clear finishes, and

then have to overlap or brush over any dried areas.

For brush cutting-in on most ceilings and walls, start in a corner and work left to right, or vice-versa. Brush on a 3-inch to 4-inch cut-in line on the ceiling or wall. Do the cutting-in on the ceiling and wall at the same time if you are using the same kind and color of water-based flat paint for both the ceiling and wall. Try to become ambidextrous so you can cut-in as far as either hand can reach to the left and right before moving your position.

Try to brush with rhythm, at a certain up-beat pace, using steady, even strokes. Always lift the brush up gradually at the end of each stroke. Use your wrist mostly and not your arms and shoulders.

Paint with the tips or face of a brush and not the sides. Painting with the sides of a brush may ruin the brush bristles. When your brush touches a surface, it should usually be at about a 45 degree angle.

To brush a straight line on an open area, you can use a straightedge and pencil, or a chalk line and mark the line first. Consider approaching the line by brushing a parallel line an inch or so away from it. Then, as you attempt to do your next straight cut-in line, you have a smooth wet paint track to guide your brush. Working the paint through the bristles of the brush with some pressure from your fingertips will produce fine and exact cut-in lines.

Instead of applying paint to a surface and brushing it out every time you apply it, consider what sometimes is a faster, better brushing method. Put about three or four short quick poking strokes of paint on a surface, separating each by about two to four inches. Then after the last daub is applied, you simply brush all the paint out smoothly and repeat the process.

Brushing is harder to do on hot days when temperatures are above 81 degrees. Hot days usually make paint-thinning necessary to get rid of snags and to have better leveling and flow. On very hot or sunbaked surfaces, brushing is not a good idea. Wait until the sun is not directly shining on them. When brushing strokes are stiff, sticky, or non-flowing because of your paint, it may be time to thin it a bit.

Clean your brushes at the end of every work day instead of leaving them in the paint or thinners. Brush bristles usually curl up after they have rested in a bucket or can for a long time. Failure to clean a brush completely by not getting all the paint and dirty water or mineral spirits out of it can cause the brush to "finger" when it dries. Aluminum foil or magazine and newspaper pages can all be folded up and used to wrap and store brushes, if you lose the original keepers. Don't leave a brush too long in paint or other chemical solutions directly exposed to sunlight. Don't leave any brush you're painting with lying across the top of a can for too long, especially in direct sunlight.

Paint remover, lacquer thinner, and linseed oil, when used separately, can help bring back some brushes to useful service again, whether by soaking or cleaning or both.

Don't stir paint with a brush. Don't use too wide a brush to paint gutters, pipes, rails, and so forth as the bristles may "fishtail" and become ruined. Don't jab a good quality brush into a vent, screen, or corner as it may ruin the bristles, causing "haywiring" to occur. The bristles get tangled, ruining them for quality work. *See also* **Brushes, Ceilings, Clear coatings, Clean-up,** and **Enamels.**

Buckets (or **pails**) come in different sizes. There is the 1-gallon bucket, called a *gal.* There is the 2-gallon bucket, called a *deuce.* And there is the 5-gallon bucket, called a *five* or *fiver.* Buckets usually come in steel, aluminum, plastic, and paper. Recommendations are for the aluminum buckets for 1- and 2-gallon sizes. Thick plastic buckets are recommended for 5-gallon sizes.

Paper buckets are for throwing away; don't reuse them. One-gallon buckets can be bought at paint stores, or empty gallon paint cans, with or without the rims, can be used as 1-gallon buckets. Two-gallon buckets usually must be bought new. Five-gallon buckets can be bought, but most of them are recycled from bulk paint cans. By the way, many so-called fivers are really 4 gallons and a 100-and-some-odd ounces, not a full 5 gallons.

Don't try to use a brush that's too big for the can: a 3-inch brush will fit a 1-gallon can, a 4-to-6-inch brush or 7-inch roller will fit a 2-gallon can, and a fiver has room for almost anything.

If you leave the rim on a 1-gallon paint can instead of removing it, consider putting four or five drainage holes in the rim with a hammer and nail, so that the paint will drip back into the can when you wipe your brush across it. The holes will not compromise the seal of the lid, if you have to store unused paint.

Always remove all paint from a bucket after using it; then clean it with the appropriate solvent. Otherwise, dried paint will build up in the bucket. When you clean a steel bucket with water, remember to wipe it dry, or it will rust.

An empty 5-gallon paint bucket can make a handy step stool. Just turn it upside down and slide it into place—very portable.

Putting drainage holes in a paint can

Burning: *See* **Blow torch.**

Burnishing is what takes place on a material or surface when it is rubbed and smoothed. Burnishing can be effective in removing spots, glares, raised grains, and defects in a wooden surface. Burnishing is also the general act of putting a luster, or gloss, on a surface by rubbing it.

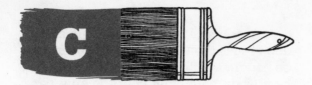

Cabinets: Most cabinets are finished in an enamel or a clear finish. My recommendation is not to use a flat paint or solid-body stain on cabinets. The important thing to remember for fine enamel work is to use an enamel undercoater first. When brushing cabinets, paint the frame around and between the doors first, then paint the doors. If a roller is used on cabinets, it's a good idea to go over the wet finish with a quality brush. However, short-nap rollers produce a stippled texture that some folks like.

It is usually easier to paint cabinets with the handles removed. Also, consider whether it might be easier to paint cabinet doors if they are taken off. It is a good idea to finish the ceilings and walls before finishing the cabinets.

If you have a lot of cabinets to paint, consider spraying them, especially if it is a new construction job or where two or three paint coats are to be applied. A sprayed enamel or clear finish on cabinets is probably the smoothest and best-looking finish.

Calcimine paints look like white-wash and usually contain zinc-oxide, water, glue, and coloring matter. These kinds of paints were used years ago on interior ceilings and some walls. When warm water combined with scrubbing or rubbing takes paint off of older interior surfaces, the rubbed-off paint is probably a calcimine paint. Paints and undercoaters don't adhere well to calcimine paints. It's essential to remove them before painting over the surface they are on. Use a strong T.S.P. solution mixed with water and a lot of elbow grease. Then undercoat the ceilings and walls with a masonry conditioner or a translucent surface bonder mixed together with an appropriate paint for a primer coat.

Carpets: First and foremost, don't get paint on carpet! Always cover a carpet with the cleanest and thickest drop cloth around. Putting clean plastic sheeting under a thick drop cloth will give maximum protection against spills. It is not a bad idea to tape a drop cloth or plastic sheet to the baseboards.

One of the most common painting mistakes is getting roller overspray and cut-in lines on carpets. A paint shield or a "painter's comb" to press the carpet down while cutting-in around carpets can help. Masking tape can also be used on carpets when cutting-in baseboards. Remember, it is a lot easier and less costly to cover and keep a carpet covered than to try and clean paint off a carpet, especially if it has dried. Anytime you can paint before carpeting is laid, do it!

Sometimes, despite your best effort, paint does end up on a carpet. You should clean it up as soon as possible. If it's a water-based paint, use dry rags to soak up as much paint as possible and then use soap, water, and gentle rubbing to clean up the rest. Keep flushing the spill area with water until the spill is cleaned up. It is important not to waste any time in cleaning up a paint spill, or the paint will saturate the carpet, or worse yet, dry and harden. On oil-based paint spills or drips, mineral spirits, turpentine, lacquer thinner, and paint remover can be used. Again, prompt attention is important. Warning: Some carpets will spot or change color from these chemicals. If you've changed the color of a carpet, or a spill has hardened in it, the entire carpet may have to be replaced. Remember to cover carpets up well and be aware of where your paint materials are at all times. If you're really careful and lucky, you will never have to use this information.

Casings: The frame or trim work around most doors and windows is referred to as a casing. Casings are usually finished in semi-gloss or gloss enamels, or in clear finishes. People tend to brush up against and get their hands on casings, so it's best if the surface is durable and easy to clean. Also, enamel casings contrast nicely with flat walls, producing a dressy look whether the colors are the same or not.

When two different colors from connecting rooms meet at a door casing, it is a good idea to paint the middle stop moulding the same color as the rest of the trim casing that shows when the door is closed. Put the other color on the other side of the casing and on the side strip of the stop moulding, but not overlapping the face of it.

All areas of casings should be treated as if they'll be under a spotlight or at eye-level. Areas on casings that weren't sanded smooth and holes and cracks that weren't caulked are easily noticed. Brush marks, lap marks, roller stipple, and holidays (missed spots) show up, too. Don't flood a casing with paint, or it will drip down onto carpets, tiles, and corners of window sills.

Caulking compounds seal cracks and crevices, providing protection against wind and water. Some are more flexible than others, depending on the application they were designed for. When they were first developed in the 1940s, they were oil-based. Today, most caulking compounds have latex in them and are better than the old oil-based ones. They are inexpensive, flow easily, set-up just fine, and are usually designated for either exterior or interior use.

Most joints, gaps, and cracks under $1/4$ inch wide or deep can usually be caulked. Sometimes two or three passes are needed on deeper or wider cracks. Most cracks and holes over $3/8$ inch should usually be patched with other materials, such as spackle, quick-patches, and the like.

Some latex-acrylic caulking compounds have silicone added to make them more mildew- and water-resistant. Some of these caulks are guaranteed to last from ten to fifty years. They are more expensive, but they are well worth the extra cost.

You can also find, usually at stores catering to the marine trade, polyurethane caulking compounds that are durable against joint movements and are quite resistant to moisture and water problems. They take longer to dry than other kinds of caulking compounds and are usually more expensive.

Clear silicone caulking compounds are available for use on and around clear finishes, semi-transparent stains, and wood preservative finishes. These clear caulking compounds resemble a gel-like plastic solution when first applied and are firm, clear, and rubbery when dry. They resist water and wind quite well. Apply a clear caulking compound after the finish is applied and has dried, unless a particular brand's label says differently.

Caulking compounds come in different colors, such as white, brown, red, and black. Don't use an interior caulking compound outside. Make sure you first read the label of the caulking compound you want to use to see if the paints you intend to apply over it are recommended. Although some caulking compounds say on their labels that they can be painted over immediately after they are applied, waiting fifteen minutes or longer is recommended for best results. Remember to remove all excess caulking from around the crack or hole, or you'll notice the difference in texture after the area is painted.

Don't apply caulk over tar or asphalt surfaces, or the caulk will deteriorate.

Caulk is applied with a caulking gun. Pull the plunger rod all the way back, slip the caulking tube into the gun, and snug up the plunger rod. Next, snip the snout

Applying caulking to the bottom of a window with a caulking gun

of the caulking tube at a slant with a knife or razor blade to produce a ¼-inch opening. Use a long nail, wire, or similar poker and jab it through the snout until it has broken the seal and has caulking material on it when you bring it back out. Next, turn the plunger rod with the teeth up and set the gun snout so it's pointed into the crack with the snout opening parallel with the crack or joint. Pump the trigger until the caulk begins to flow and move the snout along the crack or joint in one direction, making a uniform bead of caulking. At the end of your line, immediately disengage the plunger rod to stop the caulk from flowing. Smooth out the caulking bead with your forefinger before it has set-up and dried, and then wipe off the excess caulk on the surface area with a rag. Don't wipe the excess caulk on your clothes or skin. It's annoying when it hardens, and it's not very easy to remove.

Most people prefer to pull rather than push a caulking gun along a crack. It takes a little practice and experience to caulk fast, accurately, and with the right pressure release.

Some paint stores stock rechargeable automatic hand-held power caulking guns that allow you to caulk more easily for long periods of time.

Caustic soda is another name for sodium hydroxide, or lye. It is used to remove paint. Use it with caution, as it can severely burn skin and eyes. Always wear gloves and goggles when working with it. *See* **Paint remover.**

Cedar is used commonly for wood shingles and exterior trim. It is very porous and not very resinous; therefore, oil-based stains and wood preservatives penetrate it deeply. Use denatured alcohol, diluted 50 percent to 70 percent in water, to remove dried water stains on bare cedar before staining. If a flat or enamel finish is going to be used on bare cedar, first use a strong undercoater or sealer.

Ceilings: The ceiling of a room should be painted first to avoid spattering paint on freshly painted walls. This is especially important when the ceiling and walls are different colors. Also, it is easier to cut-in a straight line where ceiling and walls meet after the ceiling is painted. Always paint a room from top to bottom.

To produce the best results, work crosswise rather than lengthwise when rolling a ceiling. Remember to rest your

Use a long-pole roller to paint a ceiling.

neck periodically. Long-pole rollers, stilts, and planking often make more sense than ladders for ceiling work.

Beamed ceilings are often left unfinished, but beams can look good painted, stained, or coated with a clear wood preservative.

Cement: *See* **Concrete.**

Chain-link fencing: *See* **Fences.**

Chicken wire with a black paper baking is ideal for providing a foundation for patching-compounds when filling large plaster and wallboard holes. *See* **Holes.**

Chimneys: Most chimneys can be prepped, undercoated, and painted like any other masonry surface. To make a chimney stand out, paint it a different color than the exterior walls next to it.

Be careful when painting an exterior chimney from the roof. Make sure before climbing your extension ladder that the ladder won't slide out from under you. *See* **Masonry** and **Paint.**

Clapboard: Spraying is usually the best way to paint clapboard. (*See* **Spraying.**) If you choose not to spray it, however, the next best method is to use a 7-inch roller set-up and a 3- or 4-inch brush. Set up a planking system along one side of the house (*see* **Planking**); you will start painting at one corner under the eaves.

It is best to paint three or four courses from one corner to the other, then lower the planking system and paint the next three or four courses, and so on. The trim is painted after the siding is finished.

Begin by painting with your brush the bottom edges of three or four courses for about 4 to 6 feet, and then roll or brush the faces of the courses for the same

Paint the underside of each clapboard first, then the face.

length. The distance you paint will vary depending on whether you use enamel or flat paint or a solid-body stain, how fast you brush, and how fast your paint sets up. Since flat paints and solid-body stains leave no lap marks when applied evenly, you can paint the courses for as much as 12 feet if you want. With enamels, however, stay within the 4 to 6 feet limit, as tacking up and lap marks can occur if you get too far ahead of yourself. *See* **Exteriors, Prep work, Rolling,** and **Brushing.**

Clean-up: To judge how professional a painter is, you need to see how well he or she cleans up. Tools, brushes, and work areas should be cleaned every day. Some people never clean their brushes, rollers, or tools. Some set the brushes in water or mineral spirits, and six months later the same brushes are still sitting there, all dried out.

Begin cleaning up by stopping at a good place to "square up." End at a corner, if possible, or at least at a door or window, where any paint differences will be least noticeable. Next, put all the paint back in its original containers. Use brushes to lick out the paint from the buckets you were using. Scrape as much paint as possible from your brushes into the original containers, and put the lids back on.

If you are not going to use the paint for more than twenty-four hours, hammer the lid down securely so a skin doesn't form on the top of the paint. To keep

Use a rag to prevent paint from spraying and a hammer to secure the lid when closing a can of paint.

paint from spraying, put a rag over the lid before hammering. If you are not going to use the paint for two weeks or longer, label the can with masking tape, giving the color and type of paint and where it was used. It is a good idea to put a piece of some sort of plastic sheeting or sandwich wrap on the top of the paint rim before putting the lid down to help keep air out of the can. After putting the lid down securely, turn the paint can upside down for ten seconds or so and then turn it upright again. This action will help seal the can and keep a skin from forming.

Now it's time to pick up all your tools and clean them. Get a clean container and fill it with the right kind of solvent, either water or paint thinner. Start by working the brush bristles against the bottom of the container, lifting and squeezing them between your forefinger and thumb. Work the thinner and paint through the bristles of the brush, dipping it up and down in the thinner several times. Do all the brushes first in the same "dirty thinner" and then spin them with a spinner, twirl them between your hands into a 5-gallon empty container, or rap them on the toe of your work shoe.

For the second washing, use a clean container and the appropriate clean solvent. When no more paint comes from the base of the bristles when they are squeezed, the brush is clean. Get the remaining thinner out of it, then put it in a keeper or similar brush holder. Generally speaking, no more than three washings are usually needed to get brushes clean.

On heavily used brushes, try a wire brush to remove paint from bristles during the first and second washings. Brush in the direction of the bristles. If you still cannot get dried paint off, brush against the bristles.

When cleaning a brush with a hose or under a faucet, separate the bristles with your fingers while the water is running.

Brushes used in oil-based paints, whether cleaned or not, can be left for a while if you first drill a hole through the top of the handles and suspend them in thinner. The bristles should be completely submerged but should not rest on the bottom of the can. Or you can tie a stick to each one of the brushes so that the sticks are longer than any of the bristles at the bristle end by a inch or so, and then prop the brushes in thinner. These two methods prevent a brush from "curling."

Don't soak brushes for more than a few hours in water or the wood may swell and the ferrule may loosen when the wood dries. Some stubborn water-based paints that won't wash up with water will respond to a bath of lacquer thinner and then a clean-water rinsing. A

Try using a wire brush on the lip of a 5-gallon container to clean heavily used brushes.

handle. Do this by running the tool up, down, and around the cover, applying firm pressure as you do. It is a good idea to do this first step over the paint can you were using.

If you're returning to work the next day, you can soak the roller in the proper solvent or wrap it in a plastic bag and aluminum foil, and keep it out of the sunlight, air, or heat. But don't leave a roller like this for more than twenty-four hours.

For a thorough cleaning, pull the roller cover off the handle and clean the handle thoroughly in the proper solvent. Use a five-gallon can or a sink to clean rollers that were used in water-based paints. Use a fiver (not a sink) to clean rollers used with oil-based paints. Begin by soaking the roller cover and then wringing it out. Grip it in both hands, one on top of the other, and turn your hands to the right and left, back and forth, squeezing at the same time. Then dip the roller cover back in the cleaning agent and repeat these steps over and over. Change the cleaning agent when it gets dirty. Generally speaking, two or three changes of clean thinner are needed to thoroughly clean roller covers.

From time to time when cleaning a roller cover and after the last dip, use a spinner to spin out the roller cover in an empty fiver until only the cleaning agent comes out. Get all of the leftover cleaning agent out of it before storing it to prevent the roller cover from hardening later and becoming useless. Store it standing on end for quicker drying and to prevent matting.

Before you leave your work area, put everything in order. Fold up all the drops. Gather all the ladders and group them together. Remember that oil- and thinner-soaked rags can spontaneously combust if left in a pile. Either hang them out to dry or keep them submerged in water until you dispose of them properly. Then walk around your workspace to see if you missed anything. *See* **Brushes, Rollers, Buckets, Trays,** and **Spraying.**

bath of lacquer thinner also works well with stubborn oil-based paints. Specially packaged paint-brush cleaners, found at most paint stores, can also clean up stubborn water-based and oil-based paints on brushes.

Some painters dip their clean, dried brushes in motor oil or linseed oil. Then the brushes are spun out and stored. This keeps them supple. However, if you do this, remember to get the oil out of the brushes before using them. You don't want to mix this oil with the paint you are applying.

To clean rollers, first use a roller comb, 5-in-1 tool, or putty knife and get as much of the excess paint as possible off the roller cover while it is still on the

Clear coatings include plastic coatings, varnishes, polyurethanes, unpigmented lacquer, linseed oil, tung oil, shellac, wood preservatives, and certain wax polishes. Clear coatings are not pigmented paints. Sunlight penetrates them, so they are not recommended where they're exposed to sunlight, unless they include UV (ultraviolet) absorbers. Without these, clear finishes exposed to the sun can crack, bubble up, and prematurely deteriorate. Clear coatings with UV absorbers resist yellowing, and are more durable, but they still will not handle sunlight as well as pigmented paints.

Most clear coatings used on exterior homes or buildings should be recoated on a yearly basis, or sooner, if the house or building is near water. Don't use any clear finish outside that doesn't say on its label that it is for exterior surfaces. Don't use a flat or enamel paint directly over a clear finish. Instead, remove the clear finish and apply the right undercoater first. Also remove a clear coating before staining the wood it is on. *See* **Paint remover.**

When you want a natural, wet, see-through look on wood or some other interior surface, consider using a clear finish on it. Clear finishes provide protection and enhance the appearance of wood. Wetting a surface down with water will show you what it will look like when a clear finish is applied.

Varnishes are the hardest films, affording good resistance to water and alcohol. They enrich the color of wood, making it look warmer. Because they dry relatively slowly, dust can be a problem with varnishes. Synthetic varnishes such as polyurethane offer the most protection against scuffing and abrasion. Spar varnish is formulated for outdoor use; it is more flexible than other varnishes and thus better handles the expansion and contraction that comes from alternating temperatures and from moisture-related wood movement.

Lacquer is a fast-drying clear coating that is usually best sprayed on. But brushing lacquers can give a good, colorless, water- and alcohol-resistant film.

Clear shellac has no alcohol resistance, because alcohol is its solvent. Nevertheless it is a good, quick finish for many surfaces; just don't use it on a bar top!

Many clear finishes come in matte, flat, satin, semi-gloss, gloss, and high gloss. They're all basically the same stuff, with the lower gloss produced by particles suspended in the finish. Several coats of a low-gloss finish can therefore look cloudy. One way to adjust the sheen of a clear finish is by rubbing it out. A fine abrasive like pumice or rottenstone mixed in linseed oil will dull a sheen; wax will increase it.

Oil-based tints can be used to color oil-based clear coatings, but experiment first with small portions to see if they dissolve and how they look. Oil-based semi-transparent stains can be used in oil-based clear coatings, but don't use more than a third of them by volume. A few companies specializing in refinishing products now carry a new product that is a polyurethane and semi-transparent stain in one package, for one-pass application.

Clear coatings are a little less forgiving than pigmented paints, especially flat pigmented paints, so applying them requires extra care. It is a good idea to first vacuum the surface and the room where you're working. On interior fine custom trim and refinishing work, wipe the surface with a tack cloth before applying a clear finish. Clear finishes don't look good over porous surfaces, so consider using a sealer and perhaps a paste wood filler underneath. *See also* **Floors.**

Clear coatings don't require much mixing, because their chemical makeup is compatible, unlike emulsion paints. Don't agitate a clear finish; you will introduce air bubbles and then you'll have to wait for them to clear before you can use it. However, always make sure you get any and all the stuff stuck to the bottom of the can mixed in. *See* **Boxing.**

Brush a clear finish carefully. Scraping a brush containing a clear finish on the rim of a paint bucket can cause air bubbles to form. As mentioned earlier, a wire stretched across the opening of the bucket or can makes a better surface to rub your brush against.

Sometimes when minute particles or dust lands in your clear finish, you can remove them with a small sable artist's brush. In some cases extra-fine steel wool can be used to feather in an already dried touched-up area.

Use thin coats when spraying or brushing on clear coatings. Two thin coats are better than one thick one. Rollers are not recommended except on floors. If you do use a roller, a low-nap (3/8-inch lambswool) works great. If you are spraying on the clear finish, check what size spray tip is recommended for the specific coating.

If a dried clear finish gets small blemishes or paint spots on it, try rubbing it with a clean, non-abrasive rag dipped in a 50/50 solution of linseed oil and mineral spirits. It's seldom necessary to strip a finish because of minor problems. *See also* **Sanding sealer, Refinishing, Lacquers, Thinners, Spraying, Linseed Oil, Brushing, Oil finishes, Stains, Woods, Floors, Paint remover,** and **Paint.**

Closets should be treated like small rooms: Paint the ceiling first, walls next, and then apply enamel to any shelves, baseboards, and so forth.

Most of the prep work is likely to involve sanding the shelves and trim work and cleaning with a T.S.P. solution. Sometimes there's caulking and/or spackling, too.

Before painting, remove the clothes rod if possible, as both the closet and the rod will be easier to paint. Paint the rod with an enamel or clear finish for good protection, or leave it bare so it won't chip later.

If there are a lot of closets to be done, it may be practical to spray them. However, a 7-inch roller and brush work well, too. If you want the natural grain of the wood to show, consider using a clear finish instead of leaving the surface bare and unprotected.

Closets are a good place to break in a new or inexperienced painter. Be sure you are providing good ventilation while painting inside a closet. If practical, have a fan going.

Coal-tar enamels are made from coal-tar pitch, with mineral fillers added. They are used as a coating to keep underground steel pipes from deteriorating. Unless the temperature gets below -10 degrees or above 150 degrees, a steel pipe painted with coal-tar enamel will last a long time. The fumes of coal-tar enamel are not pleasant or healthy. Protect yourself from them with adequate ventilation and a carbon-filter mask.

Coatings: Generally speaking, you can put all the finish coats of paint you want on a surface, provided you apply the coats properly, and the previous paint coat has had plenty of time to dry. However, after three coats of paint on new construction, and two coats on most repaints, most surfaces don't need any extra.

Color: Give careful consideration to color before applying a drop of paint. If you're painting for other people, make sure they understand it's their decision, because they're the ones who will live with the color. It is worth the time and effort to make sure your client is happy with the colors chosen before proceeding. Dissatisfaction later can be complicated and costly.

Color is affected by the kind of light it's viewed under: tungsten light bulbs are relatively orange, fluorescent light is green, and daylight, depending on the time of day, can be blue or red. Color samples, or "chips," should therefore be viewed in the same light as in the area to be painted. Colors are also affected by the colors around them—another reason to study color in context. Keep in mind that a small chip will generally look lighter than the same color applied to a large area. If you can't decide on two shades of the same color, it's usually safer to choose the lighter one.

Colors affect us subjectively. Light colors make things look larger, dark colors smaller. Warm colors make things feel closer, cool colors more spacious. Colors can complement one another to create a feeling of calm and harmony, or they can contrast to create interest and energy. Colors can be used to call attention to things or to subdue them. Remember that paint does not usually account for the only color in a room or a landscape. Often you choose a color to relate to things in the foreground or background that are not painted.

If an area is too narrow in appearance, consider using warm colors on one or two of the shorter walls. If an area looks too small, consider cool pastel colors. If an area looks too large, choose warm deep colors. If an area is too square-looking, try painting one wall one color and the other three walls another color. If a ceiling is too high, consider a deep color on it. If a ceiling is too low, use pure white or a very light pastel.

Light colors are more reflective than dark ones, as follows:

• White reflects 70 to 90 percent of the light striking it;

• Off-white and creams reflect 55 to 70 percent;

• Most other colors reflect 3 to 18 percent;

• Black reflects 1 to 4 percent.

At a paint store, colors are either *custom* or *stock*. Custom colors are mixed at the store according to manufacturer's formulas. These are more expensive than stock colors, and they're usually nonrefundable and nonreturnable. You must therefore estimate usage more accurately. With stock colors, you can buy extra and return the unused, unopened cans. When buying stock colors in quantity, make sure all the cans have the same batch number. It's also a good idea to ensure against variation by mixing cans during a job, rather than finishing one before opening another (*see* **Boxing**). With any paint, always check before applying it to make sure it is the right color.

You can also mix your own colors from bases (light, deep, or ultra-deep) and tints. Make sure the tint is compatible with the base, especially that they're both either water-base or oil-base.

Black *shades* a color, white *tints* a color, and black and white mixed together *tone* a color. To tint a color is to "let it down." To tone a color is to "dirty it" or "muddy it up." If you're trying to match a color, look at and into it to see what tints appear to have been used in making it.

When mixing colors, start with a fourth or fifth of the whole amount of paint to be mixed. This way if you overshoot, you still have plenty of your base paint to get back on track. Always employ a light hand when adding tints to paints. Add a little bit at a time, remembering that you can always add more. Keep in mind that it is easier to tone or darken a color than it is to lighten it. Undercoaters, primers, and sealers are all good materials to learn color-mixing with.

Columns and pillars: For columns about 12 feet high, a 6-foot ladder and an extension ladder are usually needed. Be cautious with your extension ladder on round surfaces. It is a good idea to rope it securely and position blocks of wood or bricks at the feet of the ladder to keep it from slipping. If several columns together need painting, consider using scaffolding, or a plank-and-ladder set-up to make the prep work and painting easier on your feet and back. A plank or a scaffold will probably be safer, too.

Remember to spread plenty of drop cloths all the way around the columns you are prepping or painting. The higher you are, the farther away paint chips and drips will fall.

Most columns are painted white or off-white. A semi-gloss or high gloss exterior enamel is recommended.

Commercial jobs involve painting new office buildings, industrial plants, shopping centers, tract homes, and the like. Commercial jobs are much more competitive than custom repaint jobs on homes. A commercial job can run from thousands to millions of dollars. Most commercial jobs are done by large painting contractors.

If you ever bid on a commercial job, keep in mind that many a painting contractor has lost his shirt bidding way too low.

Concrete: Allow new concrete 60 to 90 days to age or cure before painting over it. New or unpainted concrete should be roughed-up with a wire brush to add tooth for a better bond between paint and concrete. Alternatively concrete can be etched with a hydrochloric acid and water solution (25 percent to 35 percent acid), which will also remove lime and salt deposits and keep the paint from peeling and bubbling later.

On new concrete, prime with a masonry conditioner. Most concrete is quite porous, so use a relatively thick, 1-inch-to-1¼-inch roller cover, working the paint into the pits, crevices, and pores. Two or three coats of paint are generally needed on new or repainted concrete for the best look and durability.

Epoxy and rubber-based finish paints work well for protection on interior concrete surfaces. Latex paint can be used on concrete also. *See also* **Masonry** and **Paints.**

Contract painting: The laws vary from state to state, but to be a licensed paint contractor usually requires three to four years experience, as well as insurance, bonding, and passing a test. There are contractor's schools that guarantee you will pass the state test if you give them the money to attend their classes.

The chief advantage of being a licensed contractor is that you can legally bid on all painting jobs, especially large, commercial jobs. Many people regard you as more credible, reliable, and established if you are a licensed contractor. You can put a lien on a house or building if people refuse to pay you for work already done. Having a license, however, says nothing about the quality of the work a painter does.

Copper: Most copper surfaces are not painted, but there are exceptions, such as copper gutters and downspouts and certain ornamental fixtures. Unpainted copper surfaces can be cleaned with a mixture of 12 ounces to 16 ounces of copper sulphate and a gallon of clean water followed by a thorough clean-water rinse. Make sure any undercoater that is going over copper says on its label that it can be so used. Prior to applying a clear finish, consider roughing the surface with fine- to medium-grade steel wool. Exterior clear finishes such as spar varnishes can be used to brighten up an unpainted copper surface.

Copper sulfate is a blue, crystalline, copper salt, also called blue vitriol. It is moderately toxic.

If you have galvanized iron surfaces and don't want to wait the recommended six months or longer to paint them, you can prep them with a solution of eight to ten ounces of copper sulfate in a gallon of water. Then clean and rinse thoroughly with water. Wear protective clothing and safety goggles and avoid skin contact.

Cost: If you are painting full-time, or are otherwise using a lot of paint, you should qualify for a ten to twenty percent discount at a paint dealer. Some paint companies give up to a forty percent discount for high-volume business. Usually all that is needed to qualify is a business card. Once you have a paint discount at one dealer, you can usually get one more easily at another; such is the nature of competition.

You get what you pay for in finish-painting labor. For custom work don't hire the cheapest painter around, as you may end up with a slop artist. Sometimes you can find cheap labor for the hard prep work, but many of these guys are late for work, do inferior work, and quit when they get their first paycheck. It's often more hassle than bargain.

Cracks: When flat wall paints are to be the finish on a surface with hairline cracks, caulking usually suffices. On most surfaces where enamel is to be the next finish-paint coat, putty the hairline cracks instead so that "flashing" doesn't occur. If spackle or any other patching compound is used, let it dry, then seal it with a shellac primer or stain killer before painting. Otherwise you're likely to get a different texture or sheen over the patch. *See* **Flashing.**

For cracks caused by a house settling on its foundation, nylon mesh tape is sometimes used in conjunction with patching compounds or mixes. There are also elastic patching materials.

Before patching most cracks, it's best to open them up in a "dove style" or V-shape. This can be done with a triangular molding scraper, or even with a common can opener. Screwdrivers don't work well. The patching compound will fit better and last longer in a V-shape crack. Large cracks may require hammering and chiseling to get all the loose material out before patching is done on them. Plaster and stucco mixes are good first-pass materials for deep cracks. Remember to moisten a deep crack before applying stucco or plasters to it.

Always finish off a patch by leveling it flush, feathering the edges, and texturing the surface like that surrounding it. *See* **Holes, Spackle, Stucco, Plastering, Caulking,** and **Quick-setting patching plaster.**

Creosote is a yellowish to greenish-brown, oily liquid obtained from coal tar and used as a wood preservative. It's often used where wood is near water or directly on the ground, as with posts, pilings, and retaining walls. A house on or near the shore or another damp area is also a good candidate for being painted with creosote. Creosote protects against termites, fungus, and rot.

Creosote is not to be painted over except with creosote itself. Remember this before painting a home or building with creosote.

Creosote is best applied by airless sprayer. Natural brushes or other quality brushes work well, too. Don't get creosote on your skin or in your eyes! Wear an organic vapor mask when spraying it.

Before using creosote, check if there are local regulations banning its use in your area.

Cutting-in is brushing the edges of a surface, such as a wall or ceiling, the rest of which will then be painted with a roller. The purpose of cutting-in is to get at areas that a roller can't reach or to make a line where two colors will meet on a surface. On any cut-in work, use a 3- or 4-inch border to simplify rolling.

Cutting in before rolling

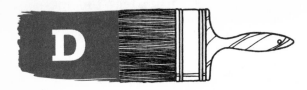

Damar is a relatively colorless natural resin obtained from trees in the Indo-Malaysian areas. It is used in making varnishes.

Decks and porches: Prep work done on new wooden decks consists mostly of sanding. Use electric sanders in a back-and-forth motion. A sanding pole works well for the sanding of overhead and side railings. Let pressure-treated wood weather for a few months before painting; otherwise, the paint will not bond well.

Because exterior decks weather and deteriorate quickly, a maintenance painting schedule of every two or three years is recommended. If you wait too much longer, you will have major prep work to do.

On new or unpainted porches or decks, a three-coat system is recommended: one coat of undercoater and two coats of finish paint. Stain finishes do not require the undercoater. Oil-based paints have good penetration and durability on wood decks and porches. It is a good idea to thin all coats of paints except the finish one. Best results come from products specifically made for decks and porches. On pool decking, consider using a special pool decking paint. These paints are expensive, but they are also durable.

Airless spraying or a roller and brush set-up are both good painting methods to use on porches and decks. Hand-brushing alone can take a long time.

New concrete decks and porches should be allowed to age seventy to ninety days before painting them. Don't use solid or semi-transparent stains on concrete decks. Rubber-based porch and deck paints work quite well on such non-wood surfaces. *See also* **Cement, Paint,** and **Wood.**

Denatured alcohol is an ethyl alcohol that is unfit for drinking because it contains methanol. It is used mostly for thinning shellac and cleaning up tools that have shellac on them.

Denatured alcohol can be used to get dried paints off windows and surfaces made of plastic and rubber on which you may not want to use paint thinners because of their fumes or the possibility that they might eat through the surface.

Denatured alcohol in a 50 percent to 60 percent ratio to water will clean up most minor dried moisture stains on woods. It can also be used as a cleaning agent after paint has been removed from wood surfaces.

Dew point is the temperature at which moisture forms on outdoor surfaces. Dew usually forms in the early morning or evening. Don't apply paint outdoors within two hours of dew time. Don't apply clear coatings outside within three hours (or sometimes more, depending on the weather) of dew time.

Doors are usually painted with high-gloss or semi-gloss finishes to make them easier to keep clean. When repainting doors, break the old gloss with sandpaper, liquid sandpaper, and/or an undercoater. If you are reapplying a clear coating, then roughing the surface is even more important. Raised grain on doors can be filled in and smoothed over with wood paste or spackle, depending on the kind of finish desired.

Before painting, either remove the door knobs or cover them with masking tape and paper. Whatever you do, don't get paint on them. Paint on a door knob can overshadow a good finish coat on the door and is very noticeable.

If you are painting the door in place, it is a good idea to leave it ajar to prevent the paint from sticking to the jamb and lifting. If you must close the door before it's completely dry, as is sometimes the case with front doors, you can keep it from sticking by applying a light coating of petroleum jelly to the jamb edges.

If you are going to paint a lot of doors, consider taking them off their hinges and labeling them so that they can be rehung without confusion. It is usually easier to take the pin off the bottom hinge first (done with a hammer and nail or screwdriver). A side benefit of taking the doors off is that the door casings are easier to prep and paint. Take the doors to a garage or other work area, lay them on sawhorses or lean them against a wall, and spray them. Alternatively, a 7-inch roller set-up and a brush is a quick method on plain, flat doors.

Molded and frame-and-panel doors are often brushed. Begin with the panel molding first, being careful not to overlap onto the outside frame. Next, finish the panel itself, and then repeat these two steps on all of your doors. Do the horizontal members (rails) next and the longer vertical pieces (stiles) last. Paint can drip or build up in the bottom corners of the panels on doors. It is a good idea to take a slightly dry brush and with the tips of the bristles brush out the excess paint in the corners before the paint dries.

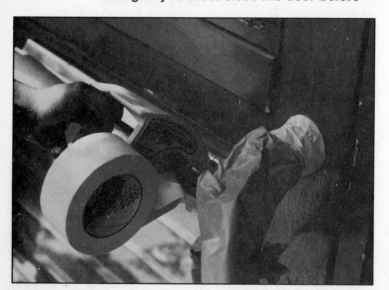

To protect door handles when painting around them, use a hand-masking machine to cover them.

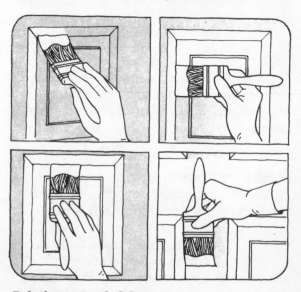

Painting a paneled door

Treat all parts of the door as being at eye level when painting them. Roller-stipple and brush marks don't look good on finished doors. Oil-based enamels are not as prone to lap marks as water-based enamels are, because they dry slower, which gives the paint more time to spread.

For added protection on doors, especially exterior ones, paint the top and bottom edges to forestall warping and splintering. However, be careful not to put too much paint on the top edge, or it will drip over onto the other side.

Remember that the jamb surfaces that contact the door edges are painted the same color as the outside of the door. Door hinges, except hinges of stainless steel or brass, are usually painted, too. *See* **Brushing** and **Prep work.**

Downspouts and gutters:
On newly installed metal gutters, it's a good idea to take some mineral spirits and wipe any oil or deposits off before undercoating them. Leave a copper gutter or downspout bare; it will develop a green patina over time. Treat wood gutters like any other exterior wood surface.

Brushing a gutter and downspout

When prepping downspouts and gutters, wire brushing, scraping, electric sanders, hand-sanding, etching, and a lot of elbow grease are typically involved.

All rust spots should be scraped, sanded, dusted, and then undercoated with a rust-resistant primer. Mildew on gutters is usually easily removed with a bleach solution.

Sometimes old, deteriorated gutters should simply be replaced. But epoxy-type cements and aluminum foil used together can temporarily fix small or medium-size holes.

Most flaking and peeling on gutters and downspouts comes from using the wrong undercoater, by not using any undercoater, or by a failure to treat or weather the original galvanized surface correctly. You must remove all loose paint completely before repainting.

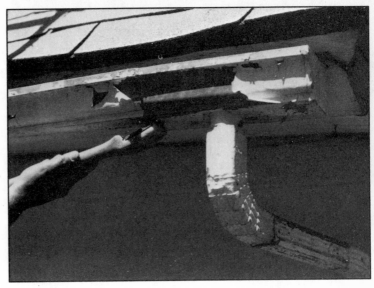

Use a large, square, four-sided scraper to help prep a badly weathered metal gutter. It is important to use the appropriate metal undercoater on gutters and downspouts before finish-coating them.

All bare metal should be undercoated. Use water- or oil-based metal primers, preferably those labeled for use on downspouts and gutters. An exterior industrial enamel or a rust-resistant enamel are good finish paints to use. Flat paints and solid-body stains are not recommended as finishes for gutters and downspouts.

A 3-inch roller and a brush work well for painting gutters and downspouts. If you brush a gutter or downspout, don't use too wide a brush, or it will "fishtail" and be ruined for quality work.

If you spray a gutter, watch out for overspray getting on the roof. It is not a good idea to lean an extension ladder against a gutter, as it may start sliding. It could also break or dent the gutter when you climb it. A gutter and downspout will be less noticeable and not seem to stand out if they are painted the same color as the surrounding area.

Clean gutters regularly to slow deterioration. Some asbestos roof coatings or gutter paints can be used on the insides of gutters to slow erosion. *See also* **Metals, Copper, Aluminum, Galvanized,** and **Copper sulfate.**

Dressers and drawers: Most painted furniture is finished in enamel because it is durable, and it looks nice. Drawer interiors and sides are generally not painted.

You can paint a dresser by sliding the drawers out an inch or so, but it's far easier to remove the drawers and position them with the fronts horizontal. You have better access to the carcase front, too. As you take out the drawers, mark them on an area that is not to be painted, remove the hardware and organize that, so you'll have no confusion when it comes time to put everything back together. Prepare the surfaces to be painted by sanding them, patching any cracks with wood putty or spackle, then sanding again.

You can paint the drawer fronts and carcase with a brush or spraygun. Don't replace the hardware or return the drawers to the carcase until the finish coat is dry and hard. *See also* **Enamels** and **Brushing.**

Drills, electric hand: Some hand drills have attachments, such as sanding discs and wire brushes, that make them useful for prep work. Also, there are paint-mixing attachments that can save time.

Drips and spills: Always use a drop cloth anywhere you are painting, and have an extra one on hand, too. Always cover objects that are not to be painted

with either masking tape or masking tape and paper or plastic sheeting before beginning to paint. Time spent up front can save a lot of anguish later on.

To avoid spills, always be aware of where your paint material is, and move methodically. Painting does not go well when you're anxious. Sometimes rushing a job will increase the chances of drips and spills.

Many dried or undried paint drips, spills, or overspray that can't be cleaned up easily with water or paint thinner will break down and clean up nicely with lacquer thinner. If lacquer thinner fails to do the job, consider using a liquid paint remover. Wire brushes combined with elbow grease work well on masonry and concrete surfaces.

A clean rag wrapped around a putty knife works well for wiping up minor wet paint drips. Pull the rag tightly, and run the putty knife and rag together parallel along an edge. Pull back, and reposition a clean part of the rag on the putty knife to wipe some more.

Over-thinning of paints will make drips more likely to occur. Applying paint too thickly on a surface will cause drips, also. Turning a roller that is loaded with paint in the air as you bring it to the surface will prevent drips from falling from it. Holding a brush with the bristles pointed down makes it more likely to drip.

Drop cloths, or "drops," are essential to painting. Always have a drop below where you are prepping or painting. Cover anything you don't want paint on, and lay drops anywhere there is even a chance of getting stray paint, prep material, or debris.

Most store-bought drops are canvas, typically white or off-white in color. They're easiest to work with because they're durable, and they don't slip around. Plastic and paper drop cloths as well as rolls of plastic sheeting (sometimes called "bisquine") are basically throw-aways, unless they don't get too much paint on them or get damaged. Old sheets, drapes, and curtains can also be used for drops. However, they are usually clumsy to move, and paint penetrates them easily. If you paint for a living, show up at the job with proper drop cloths.

Whether plastic or cloth, drop cloths are priced according to their size and thickness. Thickness is measured in "mils," which are thousandths of an inch. The larger and thicker the drop, the more it will cost, but the more use you'll get out of it. Larger cloths can be cut down for smaller jobs, especially if only part of them gets trashy. A runner is a long, narrow cloth drop. These are great for placing below doors, windows, and trim work. Runners are easy to pick up and move around.

If you paint full-time, it is a good idea to have clean drop cloths for repainting interiors. Save your semi-dirty drop cloths for exterior work and your dirtiest drop cloths for your shop area, any spray work, exterior work, or semi-transparent staining or when using patching compounds.

When moving drops or covering things, remember to keep the same side of the drops up. Also remember that plastic sheeting or drops, when covering bushes, plants, or grass in direct sunlight, can cause these living things to turn brown quickly.

Folding drop cloths by yourself is a hard way to go, so get somebody to help you fold whenever you can. The best way to fold a drop is the same as you'd fold a bedsheet: in half along the length, then again in half lengthwise until it's 2 feet to 3 feet wide. Now if there's a person at each end, they come toward one another, folding it across the width until it's 2-foot or 3-foot square. That's it.

If you have to fold a drop by yourself, spread it flat on the ground to fold. Hopefully, there won't be any wind gusts to foil your task.

Before folding a drop cloth, dispose of any loose debris, make sure the cloth is completely dry, and then shake it well. But don't shake drop cloths on lawns, flower beds, or anywhere else that stray chips are not to be desired; they're hard to pick up!

Drums: Large quantities of paint are stored in 25-, 50-, 55-, and 100-gallon drums. Unless you work for or are a big contractor, or own or work at a paint store or paint factory, you will probably never see a paint drum.

Drying: Generally speaking, a paint is considered dry when the water or thinners have all evaporated and the resins and oils have completely hardened. The paint film should be hard, not just firm to the touch. There should be no paint odor at all. A cheap paint will have a lingering odor that takes a long time to go away.

A paint-can label will indicate a drying time and a recoat time for the paint. Do not recoat a paint until the recoat time has elapsed. A paint can be dry on the outside (this is the drying time) but not necessarily completely dry where it meets the surface.

To test paint or patching compounds for dryness, always use the back of your hand, not the front of it. Feel the paint or patch as lightly as possible so as not to ruin it if it's not yet fully dry.

A primer or first paint coat dries fastest, as the solvents soak into the surface. Second and third coats take longer to dry because they sit on the surface. *See* **Paint** for specific drying times and recoat times.

Naphtha and lacquer thinners can speed up the drying time of most oil-based paints and undercoaters. Specially formulated paint driers are also available at paint stores. Use a light hand when adding these, as too much of these can mess up the paint. In hot, dry conditions, you may want to slow the drying of an oil-based paint by adding a few drops or so of kerosene.

The best weather conditions for drying paint on interior surfaces is when it is 75 degrees to 95 degrees outdoors, with low humidity, so that doors and windows can comfortably be left open. However, when applying enamels or clear finishes inside, don't allow wind gusts, bugs, and dust to ruin your nice work. Screens help somewhat. In damp places where there is little sunlight or air movement, apply thin instead of thick paint coats, or "wrinkling" may occur. Avoid painting outdoors in extremely high humidity or below 40 degrees, as this can cause drying problems and possible "wrinkling."

You can speed up the drying times of patching materials by using fans and by applying thin coats instead of thick ones.

The following are approximate drying times for various prep materials. They can vary considerably, depending on temperature, humidity, ventilation, and the thickness applied:

- New plaster (not quick-setting plasters) takes 31 to 45 days to dry before it should be primed.
- Taped drywall joints require a day or so. Last coats are typically thinner than first ones, but let them dry well before priming.
- Putty and glazing compounds used on window mullions and muntins can take 8 to 23 days to dry before priming.
- Water putty usually dries hard in 70 to 90 minutes. Quick or fast-setting patching plaster mixes usually dry hard in 10 to 30 minutes.
- Plaster of paris usually dries hard in 10 to 20 minutes.
- Stucco patch under good conditions usually dries hard in three to eight hours.

Drying oils are used in many paint coatings. The most common are tung, linseed, and soybean. There are also drying oils packaged in cans that can be bought to help oil-based paints penetrate better. They have the same benefits (and more) as mineral spirits, such as helping penetration, easier leveling and flow, workability, and the ability to reduce snagging.

Drywall, sheetrock, and wallboard are interchangeable terms for a chalky board made up of gypsum plaster encased in thick paper. Used to sheathe walls and ceilings, it is applied in whole sheets or cut to size with a razor knife and then nailed, taped, patched, and sanded.

"Dimples" are depressions in bare drywall, usually caused by the drywaller's hammer. Like the seams between drywall boards, dimples are filled with joint compound (also called mud), appropriate patching mixtures, or spackle applied with a broad putty knife. Let mud dry, as it will shrink, and then reapply. Sand lightly and seal before painting. If you don't seal mud with an appropriate undercoater or a flat latex paint, you'll notice a difference in gloss or texture.

Mud is gray in color and not as heavy or fine-grained as plaster. It goes on easily, dries in a day or so, and feathers down easily with sanding. It is a good idea to wear a particle mask when sanding drywall mud. Don't use coarse sandpaper on drywall surfaces or patches, as it will either tear the wall or cause sanding scratches to show up through subsequent paint applications. On repaints done on drywall surfaces, use spackle or quick-patching materials to repair holes and cracks.

Most new, bare drywall is undercoated with inexpensive, water-based drywall sealers, such as a PVA sealer or a latex primer-sealer. Oil-based primers are not recommended for bare drywall (but you can use an oil-based paint over a latex-primed drywall). These water-based sealers can be sprayed, rolled, or brushed on. Some types of flat interior latex wall paints can also be used for undercoating purposes. It is always a good idea to seal bare drywall before putting finish flat or enamel paints on it. Don't use a stain or clear finish on a drywall surface.

Ducts and vents: Most ducts and vents are made of some kind of metal. To make them less noticeable, paint them the same color as the surfaces around them. For more durability, always prime bare metal areas first with a good metal undercoater and finish-paint them with an enamel. Consider removing them and putting them on a drop cloth or newspaper before spraying them with an airless rig or spray can or brushing them out with a cheap brush. *See also* **Aluminum** and **Metals.**

Dust brushes, sometimes called dusters, are a necessary tool on any painting project. When doing prep or paint work, a duster should be on your person, or a step or two away. The dust brushes available at many paint stores are usually 3 inches to 7 inches in length. They are nice to use and have good bristles. However, an old, well-used natural-bristle brush that doesn't lay off well anymore is a good brush to retire from painting and make into a dust brush.

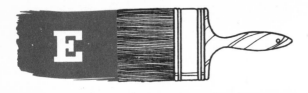

Eaves: *See* **Overhangs.**

Efflorescence is the white or light gray crystal or powdery salt deposits that sometimes form on masonry surfaces. Commonly called salting, efflorescence occurs when alkali in the masonry dissolves in migrant moisture and is deposited on the surface when the moisture evaporates. Excessive water at the base of a masonry surface can cause salting. It can also occur on interior ceilings and walls where the plaster hasn't cured properly. If such surfaces are painted, they are likely to peel.

In bad cases of efflorescence, sandblasting or water blasting may be necessary. However, try these methods for removing it first: vinegar used at full strength or a solution of muriatic (or hydrochloric) acid mixed six percent to ten percent with water. Use eye protection and avoid skin contact. Let these solutions sit five to ten minutes; then use elbow grease and a wire brush. Repeated applications are usually needed on more stubborn cases. Make sure that thorough rinsing with water removes all the salting and the cleaning solution before painting. Apply a masonry conditioner after the surface is dried completely. My recommendation is to use two coats of a good quality exterior water-based paint for the finish coats.

A water-repellent silicone sealer applied over a masonry surface can prevent efflorescence from recurring. The drawback is that this sealer should not be used over oil- or latex-based paints, unless a particular product says differently on its label.

Eggshell is a finish-coat sheen, usually of an enamel, that resembles an eggshell: somewhere between gloss and flat. Similar to a satin gloss, it is less shiny than a semi-gloss. Eggshell finishes are used mostly on interior surfaces. Paint manufacturers have different versions of eggshell sheens.

Electrostatic spray-painting employs a spray gun that electrically charges the paint particles, while the object to be painted is oppositely charged. The paint is thus attracted to the object. Electrostatic spray-painting is great for painting irregular metal objects and other metal items such as cabinets, tables, and poles. Paint tends to wrap around the object being sprayed, even when it is being sprayed from only one direction. Consequently, electrostatic spraying really helps prevent overspray from landing on unwanted surfaces or objects. For an appearance similar to that of a professional factory finish, consider finding a trained professional that does electrostatic spray-painting.

Emery cloth is a sandpaper specially suited for polishing and removing rust from metal.

Emulsions: Most water-based paints are emulsions, the pigment, resins and binder being suspended in water rather than dissolved. Oil-based paint ingredients are more mutually compatible and do not require emulsion to mix.

Enamels are technically colored varnishes. A good oil-based enamel is usually made from alkyd resins. Water-based enamels have come a long way and are getting better all the time. Some people use water-based enamels because they don't like the fumes of oil-based enamels or the clean-up with mineral spirits. Water-based enamels dry faster and thus show lap marks, brush strokes, and roller stipples more readily than similar oil-based paints. Most water-based enamels are made from acrylic or latex resins. There are also epoxy, industrial, and marine enamels, which are generally more durable than other kinds of enamels.

Enamels are well suited for trim work and some furniture, wherever you want durability, wear-resistance, and washability. An enamel on trim also adds a dressy touch to flat-painted interior surfaces. Enamels come in sheens from satin to high gloss. Enamels with more gloss to them offer more protection against the elements. Semi-gloss is probably the most popular enamel. But remember that the sheen is likely to vary from manufacturer to manufacturer; what one manufacturer means by gloss or semi-gloss may not be identical to what another manufacturer means.

Don't use an interior enamel outdoors. However, an exterior enamel can be used inside. Never mix a water-based enamel with an oil-based one! And don't mix water-based enamels with water-based flat paints, as "flashing" or "highs and lows" (differences in the surface sheen) can occur. Too much color added to an enamel with a gloss or semi-gloss sheen can cause flashing, too. Most enamels will flow better with a little thinning, especially in hot weather.

Always degloss shiny surfaces before putting an enamel finish on them. An appropriate enamel undercoater is recommended as a primer coat on interior surfaces before doing fine enamel finish work. On exterior trim work, use an appropriate exterior enamel undercoater for a primer coat to give a top-quality finish and maximum durability.

Don't use an enamel by itself as an undercoater. However, a split coat of an oil-based enamel and appropriate oil-based undercoater can be used after a previously applied and dried undercoater paint coat and before an enamel finish paint coat.

Remember an enameled surface will show defects more than a flat finish paint does, so exercise more care when prepping a surface for enameling. For best results sand any surface that is already undercoated (after it is completely dry) before putting an enamel finish over it. Tack rags are good to use on a surface before an enamel finish coat is applied for fine work.

It is a good idea to give any enamel

finish paint or enamel undercoater at least 10 percent more time to dry than the paint can label recommends before recoating.

Use natural bristle brushes with oil-based enamels for best results. Better quality enamels don't drip as much from brushes or rollers as cheaper ones do.

When applying enamel, maintain a wet edge, always spraying, brushing, or rolling toward your last wet edge. Never stop in the middle of your enameling work and let your last wet edge dry up. Instead, always finish a side, work to a corner, finish the door or window, or otherwise square-up at a good spot.

Insects can be taken out of wet enamel paint, but once the enamel paint has tacked up don't remove them. Instead, wait until the enamel dries and then remove them or sand over them and put on another coat of enamel. Keep screenless doors and windows shut to prevent insects from getting on your work on interior surfaces.

Once enamel has tacked up, don't try to correct mistakes like holidays or brush strokes, as you can do more harm than good. Instead, wait until the enamel has completely dried, and then sand it and recoat. Enamel finishes cannot be spot-painted like flat finishes when they have dried.

When enamel paint gets hard to work, sticky, or sets-up too fast, you probably need to thin it down somewhat, especially in hot weather. Kerosene and linseed oil work well in hot weather with oil-based paints. Stir enamels well and frequently in cooler temperatures and thin them a bit to make them flow and set up uniformly.

Whenever you are in doubt as to a painter's ability for fine custom work or professional painter status, all that is generally needed is to check some of his or her finish enamel brush work and it will usually tell the story. *See also* **Brushing, Rolling, Spraying,** and **Paint.**

Epoxy-based paints are newer, synthetic paints known for their toughness, hardness, strong bonding, and high resistance to chemicals, water, fungus, and corrosion. They are most often used in industrial environments on metals and masonry. They require special reducers or thinners, and they are expensive.

There are good epoxy-based rust-resistant primers available that don't require primers to be applied over them before a regular finish-paint coat is applied. Some specifically labeled epoxy paints can be used on some appliances to repaint them. Most epoxies come in gloss or high gloss sheens.

Epoxy paints can yellow and have chalking problems when they are used on exterior surfaces, so don't use an epoxy paint outdoors unless the label specifies exterior application. On interior surfaces where maximum adhesiveness and durability are wanted, consider using an epoxy paint.

Epoxy paints tack up quickly, so they require fast, skillful application. Epoxy paints, when dry, are harder to remove from a surface than most paints even when paint removers are used. So always try to wipe up epoxy paint spills or drips when they are wet. It is no cakewalk to clean up tools that have been used with epoxy paints. *See also* **Paint.**

Etching: Metals, some masonry and other materials sometimes present too smooth a surface for good paint adhesion. Therefore they are sometimes "etched" with an acid solution to give them a rougher texture, or "tooth," for painting.

For bare or unpainted concrete surfaces, a 25 to 35 percent solution of hydrochloric acid and water can etch the surface quite well. On most bare metals or aluminum surfaces, a 5 percent to 10 percent solution of phosphoric acid and water should etch the surface well and get rid of any shine.

Don't do etching in direct sunlight or on a hot surface because the etching chemicals will dry before they put a good enough bite in the surface. And remember to protect your eyes and skin when doing etching.

Extend-an-arm (also called an angle adapter) is a special tool that has one end into which a brush or scraper can be wedged. The other end has a fitting for screwing in a roller extension pole. Use this tool for hard-to-reach areas that otherwise require a long extension ladder or scaffolding and when there is just a small amount of work to be done. An extend-an-arm tool could save you the money that renting scaffolding or a special ladder might cost.

Exteriors require some special considerations. First, always use exterior paints. Varnishes and other clear finishes are not recommended on exterior surfaces because they do not block sunlight and are not durable. Lacquer stains don't penetrate well and will weather quickly. Oil-based undercoaters are excellent for use on bare wood surfaces of any kind. Penetration is important on exterior surfaces, because it provides protection, and oil-based undercoaters penetrate well.

Water-based exterior flat or low-sheen premium quality paints work well on masonry, plaster, and stucco surfaces. All exterior bare galvanized metal should be cleaned and undercoated with a specially labeled primer formulated for use on galvanized metal before it is painted.

Good-quality premium enamels, whether oil-based or water-based, in gloss, semi-gloss, or even in a satin finish, look good and protect trim longer than most flat paints. Solid-body stains and semi-transparent stains are not recommended as a durable finish for exterior trim work, as they will weather fast and provide little protection compared to an enamel finish.

Exterior prep work also requires special consideration. First don't short-change the task just because it's an exterior job; sun, water, wind, and temperature changes will test the quality of your work. Don't let paint chips from scraping or water-blasting get scattered in planting beds or garden areas; they are hard to get up completely and don't make living things grow any better. Use drop cloths, your dirtier ones when working outside, saving your clean ones for working on interiors. Paint thinners, paints, patching materials, and other chemicals should not be dumped outdoors.

Before painting or prepping, tie away from a house the trees and shrubbery that lean against it. Or cut branches away a foot or two from the house. Put drops or plastics over branches if cutting or tying them away is not practical. Vines, such as ivy, that are stuck to a surface can be removed with scraping, elbow grease, and sanding.

Generally speaking, water-blasting is one of the best ways to clean and prepare the exterior of a building before starting any other work on it.

The surface of the building is being cleaned by waterblasting with a hydroblaster, or waterblaster, in preparation for further work.

Before prepping or painting exterior masonry or stucco, it is a good idea to make the following test: Get a brass key and drag it across the surface. If it digs easily into the paint, then the surface was probably painted years ago with water-bonding cement paint. My recommendation is to remove the existing paint before painting over it. Failure to do so will usually result in peeling a short time after a finish paint has been applied. If the brass key leaves a blackish scratch, the existing paint on the surface is probably an oil-based or vinyl type of paint. To test older houses or buildings, use a scraper or a knife and scrape down to the original masonry surface, past all the paint coats. If the base masonry surface is chalky, then my recommendation is to remove all the existing paint film and then prime the bare masonry surface with a masonry conditioner.

It is not advisable to use spackle or quick-patching materials to repair masonry, plaster, or stucco surfaces. Instead, use stucco patching mixes or a patching mixture of the same stuff the surface to be patched is made of. You'll achieve longer lasting results, better looks, and a matched texture.

Use the right metal primers on all bare metal. Use rust primers on all rusted areas. Always use wood undercoaters on bare wood spots before finish-coating them with pigmented paints. Undercoat bare spots on windows where glazing or putty will go before glazing or puttying them.

Wood sidings, wood shingles, bricks, overhangs, and all rough-textured surfaces are easier and faster to do by airless spraying which penetrates all nooks and crannies. The person doing the spraying ideally should be followed by a person with a roller set-up, who can work the paint into the surface and fix all the holidays and drops to achieve a uniform finish. Two somewhat thin or medium spray coats are recommended instead of one thick one.

When preparing a metal railing, use a wire brush followed by sand-paper.

A thick coat of finish paint is not desirable on shady or damp areas such as overhangs. The long drying times in shady or damp places could cause a thick coat to flake or peel quickly. Always add a mildew retardant to exterior finish paints used in areas prone to mildew.

If you are spraying an exterior surface, watch out for overspray on the roof, cars, or nearby structures. Don't do any exterior spraying when there are strong, gusty winds. Use a spray shield to catch overspray when spraying near rooflines, around windows, and the bottom areas of exterior surfaces.

When plants, trees, bushes, or ground water are close or next to a masonry surface, the surface often absorbs the moisture or water close to it and the paint peels or the stucco falls off. Dig away the dirt from the masonry surface down to about 11 to 18 inches if possible, apply an asphalt sealer on the surface below ground level, and then patch the masonry surface above ground level with the right patching material. Remember that failure to get plants, trees, bushes, and excess water away from the masonry surface will bring back the original problem in time.

In hot weather, thin oil-based paint with kerosene or linseed oil and it will set up less quickly. For best results, don't paint in temperatures below 50 degrees or higher than 95 degrees. Painting in direct hot sunlight can cause wrinkling to occur. Nor should you paint surfaces when there is high humidity, fog, or light rain. In fact, don't paint any surface that has moisture or water on it.

Use extreme caution when working on a roof or when working from a roof to reach some other part of the house or building. In general, more caution is needed when working on ladders outside, as the ground is not as stable or level as a floor.

Whenever any part of a ladder will rest against or touch a newly dried surface, tie cloths, socks, or rags to your ladders to protect the surface. *See also* **Paint, Prep work, Masonry,** and **Wood.**

Eye-level: Among professional painters the term eye-level is important, because it refers to all work that is easily seen. Generally speaking, eye-level includes everything 3 feet up and 3 feet down from the average person's eye-level. It's easy to miss a paint holiday or bad patch job 12 feet high or near ground level. However, at eye-level it's impossible not to notice flaws. So make sure that all the eye-level bugs are out of your finish painting or patch work job before it is inspected.

Eyes are impossible to replace. Always wear safety goggles whenever doing any chipping, scraping, sanding, or when there is even the slightest chance of objects flying off into your eyes. Also wear goggles when working with acids, caustics, or bleach.

Regular prescription glasses or sunglasses are not enough protection against flying things as they do not protect from the sides or top. You can now

purchase good goggles at some paint and hardware stores that have vents on the sides to keep them from fogging.

While painting in bright sunlight or on reflective surfaces, wear sunglasses.

A **Fascia board** is the piece that runs along the entire roofline of a house or building. Most fascia boards are considered trim work, are made of wood, and are finished in enamel. Prep a fascia board the same way you'd handle other exterior wood trim work: scraping, power-sanding, hand-sanding, spackling, caulking, and applying an exterior wood undercoater to the bare spots. Fascia boards are typically exposed to the sun and to water coming off the roof when it rains and thus take a beating. Along the ocean an exterior industrial enamel or two coats of marine enamel may be in order for maximum protection and durability.

Fascia boards can be painted the same color as the house or a contrasting

To paint a one-story fascia board without using a ladder, try using the "hockey-stick brush" technique.

color. Some fascia boards have strips of metal flashing around them. This metal strip should be painted the same color as the fascia board. A 3-inch or 7-inch roller set-up and a brush are good for painting fascia boards. If you paint fascia boards by brushing only, consider using a plank and ladder set-up. A one-story fascia board can also be painted with the "hockey-stick brush" technique.

Feathering is a technique for blending a small area into its surroundings. It applies to spot-painting, spot-priming, touch-up work, and patching. Feather paint with a dry brush or dry roller, working the paint from the wet spot into the dry surrounding area. For plaster patches, use a foam float, again feathering the wet material into the dry. Aim to imitate the surface texture so that the spot is indistinguishable.

Fences: Painting a fence the same color as the walls of the building it surrounds will make the building seem more rambling and extensive. Painting a fence a different color will make the fence stand out and put the house in perspective. It can also create a confining feeling.

Make sure you lay drops around the fences you are painting or prepping. A water-blaster or common garden hose can clean a fence quite well. Use a wire brush for scrubbing chain-link fence.

The kind of material the fence is made of will determine the undercoater and finish paint to be used on it. (*See* **Wood, Stucco, Metal, Brick.**) Airless sprayers and cup guns are great for painting fences quickly. Painting a fence by brushing only could take a month of Sundays to do. It's best to use two or more people to prep and paint a fence whenever possible. The job will go faster, be less boring, and drips on both sides of the fence can be easily fixed. A 3-inch or 7-inch roller set-up (depending on the size of the fence

post or boards) and a brush are good tools to use for most fences.

Ferrous metals contain iron and, unless they are an alloy like stainless steel, are subject to rust. Even galvanized steel will rust, once the zinc galvanizing has worn off.

Fiberboard: *See* **Particleboard.**

Filler: Porous woods, such as oak and mahogany, will look more refined when finished with a clear coating if their pores have first been filled with a paste wood filler. This is a bulky paste that can be colored to match or contrast with the surrounding wood. Apply it generously, then press it in with a squeegee or putty knife and remove the excess. When it's dry, sand it flush. *See also* **Wood.**

Fire hazards: Oily or thinner-soaked rags are a fire hazard and should be kept away from open flames, heaters, and the like. They should be put outside at the end of every working day. Volatile paints such as epoxies and lacquers should be treated with caution: no smoking around them and no open flames. Electrostatic painting is a fire hazard, so keep fumes, thinners, and so forth far away from your work area. Sparks from power machines and extension cords are also potential fire hazards.

Fireplaces: Paint that gets on natural bricks or other fireplace materials may be hard to get off, so always keep the fireplace covered when painting around it.

If you decide to paint a fireplace, keep in mind that it is subject to soot, so a finish coat of enamel is recommended over a flat finish; enamel looks elegant, is easier to clean, and is more durable. At least put an enamel coat on the forehearth of the fireplace for added protection, even if the rest of it is getting painted with a flat paint.

When you paint a fireplace, whether by spraying or rolling, use a 1-inch or 1¼-inch roller set-up and work the wet paint into the nooks, crannies, and pores. *See also* **Bricks.**

Fire-retardant paints: *See* **Heat-resistant paints.**

Flagpoles: Try to paint a flagpole (or any large pole) before it is set in place and standing upright. However, if a tall flagpole is strong enough to support an extension ladder, consider tying a ladder against it. Have someone hold the bottom of it for added protection. Cover well below the flagpole and keep in mind that paint flies farther away the higher up you are. A lot of paint and overspray will be wasted trying to spray a standing flagpole or tall pole. A roller set-up with a brush are better tools to use. Consider using an industrial, rust-resistant, or marine enamel in a semi-gloss or high gloss for finish-painting a flagpole so it won't have to be repainted too soon.

Flashing is the protective metal strips that keep roof transitions watertight. Flashing around window and trim areas doesn't look very good, but it does control water runoff and fight rot. Flashing around fascia boards and other prominent places looks better painted the same color that is near it. New flashing can usually be cleaned quite easily with mineral spirits. If possible, remove any tar that the roofers may have left, using mineral spirits and elbow grease. Undercoat new flashing with an exterior metal primer before applying finish coats. *See also* **Aluminum, Metals,** and **Galvanized.**

Flashing also refers to a surface defect, sometimes called "highs-and-lows," where the sheen is not uniform. Mixing flat paints and enamel paints together will produce flashing. Improper thinning of an enamel or clear finish will produce flashing. And water or condensation during the drying time will cause a paint to flash.

Flat paint has no shine, sheen, gloss, or luster to it. Most flat finishes are used on interior ceilings and walls, and on stucco and masonry surfaces. Solid-body stains and semi-transparent stains are also flat finishes and are used commonly on wood surfaces.

One of the most common paint failures occurs when people apply a flat finish over a smooth or glossy finish. Eventually the paint can be taken off in sheets. If you must put a flat finish over a glossy surface, sand or "break" the gloss, and then apply a good, appropriate, penetrating undercoater and allow it to dry completely. Then you can apply a coat or two of a flat finish over it and not worry about paint peeling.

Flat paints are not recommended for use on interior or exterior trim areas, such as casings, windows, doors, fascia boards, gutters or anywhere else where there is a need for extra protection. Flat paints are not recommended for use in bathrooms, kitchens, laundry rooms or on cabinets, dressers, drawers, and baseboards. A flat paint used on exterior trim gives less protection than an enamel paint against water or sunlight, both of which can penetrate and cause flat paint to quickly deteriorate. Gloss paints reflect sunlight and cause water to bead. There are now available flat water-based acrylic paints that carry special limited guarantees of ten or fifteen years and that are proving quite durable. However, for greater durability on a properly prepped and undercoated exterior trim surface, the more gloss the better. Flats put on interior ceilings and walls where durability is not a major factor are more restful to the eyes than glossy surfaces.

Most flat paints, including the better ones, are water-based and made from acrylic, vinyl, or latex resins. Generally speaking, flat paints contain more pigments than glossy paints, and consequently, they tint up quite well and fast. *See also* **Paint.**

Floats are hard-backed foam tools about 5 to 6 inches wide by 12 to 15 inches long. They have a wood or plastic handle on one side. They are used mostly for floating or feathering stucco or other rough, sandy patching materials and for matching rough, sandy textures. Almost all stucco- and sandy-type textures can be feathered and matched with a float. There is usually no comparison between using a float versus using a brush or sponge for feathering stucco or sandy textures. Floats are usually available at building-materials supply outlets and at big hardware stores.

After the stucco patch or sandy patching material is put in a hole or crack, the float is used for the final pass. Start floating as soon as the patch has begun to set up.

When using a float, dip it frequently in clean water, shaking the float to get rid of the excess before using it. Apply the float to the patched area and push out in swirls, working the material out just as when you feather paints. Aim to get the patched area flush with and in the same pattern as the surrounding texture. With practice and concentration, in a short amount of time you can get good at floating patches.

Rinse a float completely when you're through floating so that the stucco or sandy texture trapped in the foam doesn't harden and ruin your tool.

On hot, dry days don't let your patch-es go too long before floating them, as they will harden and dry much faster than on cooler days. One of the nice things about floating, however, is that even if a patched area is almost completely dried, enough water, floating, and elbow grease can usually pull it out (feather it out) and float it right in.

Hard rubber floats are used by cement workers for walkways and driveways. These kinds of floats are usually not as good for feathering or floating stucco or other sandy textures on walls and ceilings as the foam floats.

Floors: On wooden floors, a floor sander, large belt sander, and a floor edger are good ways to prepare the surface. Don't sand over wax, or you will force the wax into the wood grain, making it nearly impossible to remove. Instead, use an industrial-strength wax stripper to remove the wax prior to sanding.

Before using a floor sander, make sure that any popped nails are countersunk. Begin sanding with 80-grit sandpaper and then finish sanding with 150-grit sandpaper. Make sure you or the person doing the sanding with the floor sander doesn't make swirls or indentations in the wood. Examine the floor with a mechanic's or trouble light before applying a finish. It is a good idea to vacuum floors two or three times after sanding.

Where a clear finish is desired and there are cracks or open grained wood, consider using a paste wood filler to fill in these areas before applying a finish. Use a brush and some thinner for ease and speed when applying a paste wood filler. Tinted wood putty can be used to fill in small holes or hollow areas on wood floors.

If a polyurethane or similar type of clear finish is used, check the label to see if a floor surface conditioner is recommended first. Clear shellac can be used as a primer on wood floors because it is a good sealer. On oiled wood floors, a lacquer sealer can prevent "highs and lows" from occurring (*see* **Flashing**). Floor sealers can be applied by brushing or by flooding an area and using a squeegee to soak up excess amounts. A typical seal coat consists of a 50/50 mixture of your final clear finish and the appropriate thinning agent. Apply a seal coat thinly, so that there is no glare or sheen when it is dry. After thorough drying, a seal coat should be sanded using 280-grit sandpaper to start, and finishing with 400-grit sandpaper prior to the final finishing. A seal coat will prevent semi-transparent stains from bleeding through the final coats.

Always paint in a direction that gives you an exit; avoid painting yourself into a corner! Have good ventilation for obvious health reasons and for quicker drying times. After a clear finish on a wood floor has dried for five to seven days, consider applying two coats of a paste floor wax to highlight and protect the finish.

For painting wood floors with pigmented paints, *see* **Decks and porches.**

Allow new concrete floors seventy days to cure before painting. It is a good idea to wire-brush new or unpainted concrete floors. Next, use a solution of one part muriatic acid with two or three parts water to etch the concrete for better bonding. *See* **Etching.**

Before repainting concrete floors, clean them up with T.S.P. and water; for grease spots use a degreaser. On old paints found on concrete floors (other than synthetic types such as epoxies, polyurethanes, etc.), flood the floor with paint remover and let it sit there to bubble the paint. Scrape the paint off with the biggest scraping tool you have, and repeat the procedure until no more paint comes up. How easily paint chips or sands off should determine whether or not to remove all of it with the caustic soda solution. Most concrete floors are porous, so whatever painting method is used, you should follow with a roller set-up to work the wet paint into the concrete. Two coats are the minimum on new or bare concrete floors, and three to four coats are even better.

Moisture forms more readily on concrete floors than on wood floors in similar weather conditions. So, the drying times of pigmented or colored paints is longer. Make sure moisture of any kind is completely gone from concrete floors before painting them.

Use deck paints on concrete floors instead of regular household paints. A paint with a shine or sheen to it can become slippery when wet. Consider adding a sand or texture additive. Thin your first paint coats up to 30 percent to make them flow more easily.

Remember to cut-in first when painting floors; roll last. *See also* **Woods, Concrete, Cement,** and **Paint.**

Fluorescent colors are bright and eye-catching. Many poster and sign paints are fluorescent. Fluorescent paints can have two, three, or four times the visibility of other paints. They are usually more costly than regular color paints. Some paint dealers have already-made-up stock fluorescent colors in gloss or flat finishes. For traffic areas, walkways, or to really brighten up an area, fluorescent paints can be effective. Fluorescent paints used outdoors will fade quickly before they deteriorate or weather.

It may take two or three coats of a different color and type of paint to cover a fluorescent paint. Fluorescents have a tendency to bleed through coats of paints put over them. A quick-drying stain killer is a good undercoater to put over a fluorescent color before repainting.

Formica: *See* **Plastic.**

Fumes: Paint fumes are not healthy to breathe. The most important protection is adequate ventilation. Have doors and windows open whenever practical and use fans to move air through your work area. When spraying, always wear an organic vapor respirator (*see* **Masks**); a particle mask is no substitute.

Vanilla extract and odorless thinners used in oil-based enamel paints can help disguise the smell of enamel fumes in many cases, but these are no substitute for adequate ventilation and respiratory protection. Lacquers, epoxies, enamels, wood preservatives, varnishes, polyurethanes, mineral spirits, reducers, sealers, and all oil-based paints give off unhealthy paint fumes. Water-based paints may not have bad-smelling fumes, but they are not healthy either. There are many painters who will tell you their health and lungs have been ruined by inhaling paint fumes unnecessarily or unwisely. Children, pets, and plants should not be exposed to concentrated paint fumes, either.

Paint fumes are a fire hazard, so avoid striking matches or smoking cigarettes in the area you're painting. Don't have a lit water heater, a pilot light in a stove or oven, or any sparks or flames around concentrated paint fumes, as they may cause an explosion. Oily or thinner-soaked rags should never be left in a room or near any open flames or pilot lights.

Furniture: *See* **Refinishing, Paint remover, Clear coatings, Oil finishes,** and **Outdoor furniture.**

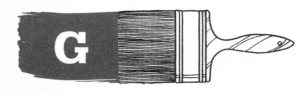

Gables: Use caution when working on slanted roofs or gables. Sometimes pulleys and ropes are needed to afford a safe stance.

Gallon: Many paint cans today referred to as a gallon actually contain less than a full 128 ounces.

Galvanized metals are ferrous metals, electroplated with zinc to inhibit rusting. When the zinc wears off, which eventually it will do, these metals will rust. A coat of paint will increase their durability.

New galvanized metal should be allowed to weather about six and a half months before being painted. If you can't wait six months to paint galvanized metal, then consider making a solution of seven to ten ounces of muriatic acid with a gallon of water; apply it to the surface and rinse it off with water. Repeat this application until all the residue is gone. Or, use eight to ten ounces of copper sulfate mixed with one gallon of water. Apply it as you would muriatic acid. Then use a metal primer that says on its label that it is to be used for galvanized metal surfaces.

To get rid of the shine on new galvanized metal surfaces, use a 5 percent to 10 percent solution of phosphoric acid. Sometimes undiluted white vinegar applied liberally will work, too.

Avoid using galvanized steel nails on wood shingles or wood fences as they will eventually rust, and then streak, and bleed down the wood. *See also* **Metals, Rust, Gutters, Ferrous,** and **Paint.**

Garnet is a hard, reddish-brown mineral used to make garnet sandpaper.

Glazing involves putting translucently thin coatings of oil, varnish, and thinner over a specially painted base, and then wiping or otherwise shaping this coating to produce special patterns, sheens or textures. The look of different woods, leather, and fabric can be simulated. *See also* **Graining.**

Glazing compound: *See* **Putty.**

Glazing points are small triangular metal plates that are used, along with glazing compound, to hold glass in a wood frame. A putty knife works well for setting glazing points into sash. Avoid hammering or violently forcing the points into a window, as you may break the glass.

Gloves: Protect your hands! Wear cloth plastering gloves or cloth work gloves whenever you chip or sand or are working around splinters or also when patching—anytime you need general protection. Also, as often as is comfortable and practical, wear lightweight gloves while painting. Long-term exposure to paint chemicals can increase your sensitivity to them. Wear rubber gloves when working around acids or paint removers or when cleaning brushes and rollers with mineral spirits, lacquer thinners, and the like. Some varieties of rubber gloves will melt when exposed to certain acids and thinners. Check the recommended application before buying.

Use throw-away cheap plastic or surgical gloves for clean-up and quick, messy jobs. Plastic gloves do get hot to work in; they also can melt and tear easily, so they're not recommended for regular use.

Glue, when added to a patching mix and to the area to be patched, creates a strong bond and makes a tight patch. For big patching jobs, buy plaster glue or cement glue found in big hardware stores and building-supply outlets. For small patch jobs, use regular white household glue. After you have chipped and cleaned out the area to be patched, apply a 50/50 solution of glue and water. Brush this solution into the entire area, with most of the emphasis on the corners of the area to be patched. Add a little glue to your patching mix; then add water and mix well. Add glue with a light hand, or the mix will be difficult to work.

Grain: When referring to wood, grain usually refers to the visible orientation of the wood cells, and it is a common understanding that sanding, for instance, should be done with, or along, the grain. So should brushing.

But grain can also mean the *texture* of wood, and it can be useful to know that water applied to wood (as in water-based paints) raises the grain. Therefore, to achieve the smoothest surface, it is a good idea to sand, dampen the surface lightly, let it dry, and then resand.

Graining is a method of application used to simulate the grain of wood on a surface. It is an art that few painters have mastered. It takes time and skill; good graining is expensive. There are books available that demonstrate graining patterns and techniques. Also, a veteran painter may be able to help. Practice first on your own interior home areas or furniture and get good at it before doing it for somebody else. *See also* **Antiquing.**

Grease must be removed before painting, otherwise it will compromise adhesion and may bleed through a finished surface. Be on the lookout for grease in kitchens near stoves and stove vents. Ammonia, T.S.P., and other detergents should get rid of most grease problems. Use a strong degreaser for stubborn stains.

Gypsum is a white material that is used to make plaster of paris, gypsum plaster, plasterboard, and wallboard. Gypsum wallboard easily starts to deteriorate and get chalky when wet. *See also* **Drywall** and **Plaster.**

Hallways and corridors: Do preparatory work and painting in a hallway just as you would any room. Paint the ceilings first, walls second, then the doors, casings, trimwork, and finally baseboards. Have plenty of lighting in a hallway, as missed spots, or "holidays," can easily occur. In other words, don't work as if in a cave just because you are in a hallway.

Hand-masking machine, or hand-masker, is a miniature version of a standard masking machine and is used for covering things that you don't want

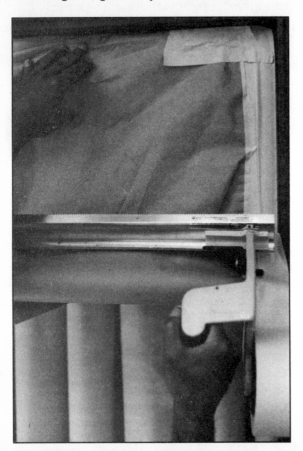

To keep paint off window panes when painting (especially when doing spraying), use a hand-masking machine to cover them.

painted. A hand-masking machine can be held quite easily with one hand while the other rips the sheets off. These machines are usually made of plastic and are relatively light. They give out just the right amount of masking paper and tape at one time, and eliminate a lot of piecing. Blades and masking-paper rolls can be easily changed. If you do a lot of spraying, a hand-masker is a real time-saver.

Hawk: a square sheet of metal with a handle underneath that a plasterer uses to hold his plaster. It's much easier to plaster from a hawk than from a bucket of patching compound, because the material is near to hand and you can control the amount on your knife.

Health and safety: Painting is not an inherently dangerous activity, but accidents can occur, and many of the materials are toxic. Accidents happen most often when you're uptight, tired, or overworked. Come to your job site well rested and ready for work, concentrate on what you're doing, and don't push yourself relentlessly. In hot weather, drink a lot of water, or better yet, citrus juices (without added sugars), which can do wonders for your stamina. Put your feet up whenever possible at break times or when you are not working. This will restore blood circulation and rest your tired back.

Be especially careful when you're working on a ladder. Be sure to keep yourself and the ladder away from electrical wires. Inspect the ladder before climbing it, and don't use a ladder that's not sturdy. Make sure it's securely planted on all four feet, if it's a stepladder, or at both the top and bottom, if it's an extension ladder. A ladder spreader at the top end, which provides wider contact with the building, makes a big difference. Extension ladders should have at least a 3-foot overlap between the two sections. Place the foot of the ladder 1

Keep yourself and your ladder away from the main electrical wiring of a house.

foot away from the building for every 7 feet of ladder height; a lesser ratio, and the bottom can slide out; a greater ratio, and you could fall over backwards. *Always* be aware of your balance and don't overreach. Keep your belt buckle within the uprights of the ladder.

Wear thick-soled rubber shoes on a ladder and try not to stand on the rungs for a long time: the concentrated pressure of the rungs can take its toll on your feet, legs, and back. When standing or crouching, keep equal pressure on your legs and feet. Take it easy when painting ceilings; relax your neck periodically. Don't work in a crouched position too long; vary your position.

Always bend your knees when lifting anything to avoid lower back problems. Don't lift awkward, heavy, or slippery things by yourself or you may get a hernia. It is better to carry a full unopened 5-gallon paint can barrel-style with both arms than to carry it with one hand only. However, if you're strong enough, two unopened full fives can be carried, one in each hand, for balance.

Wear an organic vapor respirator whenever any spraying is done to avoid getting paint spray, fumes, and particles in your lungs. Wear a particle mask when doing any sanding. Sanding dust is harmful to breathe. *See* **Masks.**

Wear safety goggles whenever you are chipping or scraping, or when there is even the slightest chance of something flying off and getting in your eyes. Wear sunglasses in sunny, bright, or reflective conditions for protection from glare.

Before eating or smoking, always wash your hands after using and contacting paints, patching materials, paint thinners, solvents, reducers, and the like.

Wear rubber gloves whenever you are doing extensive cleaning with solvents. Protect your skin from paint and solvents with a good hand lotion or gel. Hand cleaners, petroleum jellies, and shaving cream can all be used to clean hands and skin after contact with paints and paint thinners. Hand cleaners with pumice in them are more efficient.

Don't clean your face or any exposed cuts with mineral spirits or strong solvents. Follow all the cautions when using any paints or thinners, especially those labeled poisonous.

When working with acids or other harmful or dangerous chemicals, follow product directions and protect your skin, eyes, and lungs. Mix acids by adding acid to water, never water to acid, because the acid can splash up into your face. Don't mix cleaning materials, acids, reducers, thinners, or paint removers together and never mix bleach and ammonia; the resultant fumes are toxic.

When using liquid sandpaper, be sure you are in a well-ventilated area. Its fumes are very toxic.

Remember that rags, paints, undercoaters, thinners, and some building materials are all potential fire hazards. Oily or thinner-soaked rags can spontaneously combust; let them dry out before disposing of them, or keep them submerged in water.

Don't smoke, light a match, or have open flames or sparks where any oil-based paints, epoxies, undercoaters, varnishes, or wood preservatives are being sprayed. Be careful when torching or using a heat gun to remove paint.

When mixing up stucco patching mixes, protect your skin, eyes, and lungs, because the lime contained in these mixes is caustic. Wear gloves when working with any lime-based patching materials.

Always have a well-equipped first aid kit with you on a painting job. It is also a good idea to have on hand the phone numbers of the nearest hospital emergency room and poison control center.

Heaters: It is recommended to use a top-of-the-line metal undercoater as a primer coat on the painted or bare metal surface of a wall heater after any needed prep work is done. Industrial enamels, rust-fighting enamels, and fire-retardant paints are all possible good finishes. Aluminum paints can be used as a primer and finish paint coat, but the grayish color may not be desired. Don't use a flat paint, stain, or a clear coating on a wall heater. *See also* **Paints** and **Metals.**

Heat-resistant paints are special paints used on boilers, stoves, hot pipes, and the like, that will not ignite or lose their protective qualities when exposed to high or hot temperatures. They are usually enamels and aluminum-based.

Fire-retardant paints are special paints used on ships, offices, hotels, factories, and aircraft because they reduce flammability and won't ignite very easily.

Heavy hand vs. light hand: When you are mixing a color and you put too much tint in, you've used a heavy hand. Putting paint on too thickly is using a heavy hand. When you put too much thinning agent in paint to thin it, that's using a heavy hand, too. In almost all painting situations, a light hand is better than a heavy hand!

Hiding power is used to describe how well a certain paint covers over another paint or surface. Generally speaking, more expensive top-of-the-line pigmented paints have more hiding power than cheaper grades of pigmented paints.

Solid-hide is used loosely for describing either a flat wall paint, or a solid-body stain. No-hide is used loosely to describe a semi-transparent stain or a clear finish. Semi-hide describes an undercoater or a finish paint coat that doesn't cover well with the first coat.

Holes: When preparing a hole for patching, make sure you remove all loose material. Scrape out the hole with a scraper to create a shape and surface that the patching material will adhere well to.

On interior holes or cracks less than $\frac{1}{4}$ inch in diameter, caulking in a pass or two should usually be sufficient.

For $\frac{1}{4}$-inch-to-3-inch holes, spackle or quick-patching mixes should suffice in two or three passes. For 3- to 6-inch-wide holes, or any size deep holes, use stucco, plaster, or quick patch mixes, depending on the kind of texture surrounding it. If the texture is sandy or stucco-like, then regardless of the size of the hole, use stucco. For holes 6 inches or larger, stucco patch or the same plaster that the original wall or ceiling was built with should be used.

Always use a putty knife that's wider than the hole or crack to be filled. For holes or cracks 6 inches or more in size, use a plasterer's trowel.

Generally speaking, for best results don't use spackle, caulking, or quick patches on exterior masonry surfaces. However, exterior caulking and spackle can be used on fascia boards and on almost all wood surfaces and trim.

It is a good idea to dampen a hole or crack before using stucco or similar patching compounds. The patching material will then dry more slowly and also be less likely to fall out. If a hole to be patched has no backing behind it or simply goes all the way through the wall, try the following technique:

Use a dowel or wood stick longer than the width of the hole by an inch or more and a piece of chicken wire with a black paper backing, an inch or two wider all the way around than the hole to be patched. Tie the stick and the chicken wire together with twine so that the stick is a crosspiece behind the wire. Put them both in back of the hole and tie more twine to something fixed outside the hole. The hole now has a backing. Next, use stucco patch or a quick patch and do your first pass on the hole. When this patch is dried, cut the string or twine as close to the inside of the hole as possible. Then put two or three passes of patching material on the entire area. Finally, with the last pass, match the surrounding texture.

For 6-inch or larger holes in drywall, it's best to cut out an area so that you can apply a new piece of drywall onto the studs for support. Smaller holes can be filled with a piece of drywall an inch or so larger than the hole. Cut away the back paper and the gypsum center, leaving the front paper overlapping the hole. Like a mushroom, the patch will fit in the hole, and you can plaster it down with joint compound.

Stucco patching mixes can be used for texturing most sandy or stucco-type surfaces. Consider using either a flat scrub brush, a coarse-fiber brush, or a float tool to "texture-out" the stucco patching material. Use somewhat circular motions and try to match the existing surface texture next to the hole or crack. Large or extensive holes may require a professional plasterer. *See* **Cracks, Hawk, Trowel, Stucco, Float, Spackle,** and **Caulking.**

Holiday: a slang term for a missed spot on a painted surface.

Humidity and rain: Moderate to heavy humidity causes paints to tack-up slowly and to take longer to dry. This is especially true in cool, humid weather. If you must paint in high humidity on a hot day, thin your paints from time to time. Many paint stores sell specially formulated driers that can be added to paint; use these with a light hand, as they can compromise the paint's adhesion. Also, remember to wipe dry any surfaces before painting over them.

Avoid working during predictions of rain, although oil-based paint will dry in light rain, and even water-based paints may not be a problem, as they tack up quickly. However, when water does mix with undried water-based paints already applied, it can cause the paint to run, streak, or bubble. When water mixes with undried oil-based paints already applied, it can cause the paint to separate, wrinkle up, or become pitted. *See* **Drying** and **Weather conditions.**

Hydro-blasting: *See* **Water-blasting.**

Hydrochloric acid: *See* **Muriatic acid.**

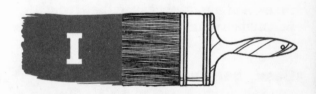

Insects such as gnats and flies seem to be attracted to relatively slow-drying materials like enamels and clear coatings. Water-based flat paints are usually not a problem. If the coat has tacked up a little but is still quite wet, a bug can be taken out of it with little or no problem. However, if your paint is almost dry and it's an enamel or clear coating, don't remove the bug, as you may mess up your finish more than if the insect stays at this point. Instead, let the paint dry completely and then remove the bug and little if any damage will generally occur.

When working outside, there is little that can be done to stop bugs from getting in your work. However, there are special paint additives that supposedly repel insects. You can also work early in the morning when there tend to be fewer insects around. When working inside, make sure there are screens on open windows and doors.

Insects such as bees, wasps, and bumble bees are attracted to wet paint. If you are scared of them or they annoy you, consider using an insect repellent.

When prepping wood surfaces such as fascia boards, sidings or eaves, be on the lookout for insect damage, especially by termites. A professional exterminator may be in order.

It is not a good idea to leave exposed an untreated wood surface. At the least apply a wood preservative, which will give some protection against insects.

Insurance: Anybody who paints for a living should have accident, health, liability, and perhaps also disability insurance. It is a good idea to shop around and compare prices and coverage. Some contractor licenses and many contracts require insurance coverage. Many home and building owners want to know that a person working on their property has insurance.

Interiors: As with any job, prep work must precede the actual painting of an interior. Don't forget to do the necessary masking, and to lay down plenty of drop

When painting a bathroom, cover the shower tile with either masking tape (bottom) or with masking tape and paper (top), both dispensed from a hand-masker.

cloths. The ideal weather for interior painting is a sunny, warm, clear day when windows and doors can be left comfortably open to get rid of paint fumes and odors and to help paints dry.

It's best to proceed from top to bottom: Paint the ceilings first, then the walls. The doors and windows are next, then the casings, dressers, drawers, cabinets, and baseboards. Painting or not painting electrical switch plates and outlet plates is a matter of personal taste. However, electrical switch plates and outlet plates should be removed during a painting operation, whether you paint them or not. If you do paint them, use an appropriate undercoater on them first and then consider using an enamel paint, instead of a flat paint, for greater durability and best results. When cutting-in, put a 3-inch or wider border on enamel-painted ceilings and walls and a 3-to-4-inch or wider border on flat-painted ceilings and walls.

Don't forget to leave touch-up paints for your clients and to mark them for future usage.

Flat paint is not recommended for interior woodwork and trim because it's not washable or durable enough on these surfaces.

When painting in a kitchen, turn off the stove pilot light. Also turn off the pilot if you are going to put a drop or plastic on top of the burners on the stove.

To figure coverage, begin with simple square footage of ceilings and walls. For a door with casing, figure 35 to 40 square feet. For a door alone, figure 15 to 23 square feet. For a window with casing, figure 35 to 40 square feet. For a window alone, figure 12 to 18 square feet.

These are only approximate figures; surface, weather, and type of paint can affect coverage. It is a good idea to get at least 10 percent more paint than what you estimate. *See also* **Brushing, Rolling, Spraying, Bathroom, Cabinets, Casings, Doors, Shelves,** and **Windows.**

painting experience, and who is considered a professional painter by other painters is called a journeyman.

Journeymen are always needed on painting jobs, especially commercial jobs, because of their speed, know-how, and skill. Journeymen earn good wages. They have a reputation to uphold, one that's been established by generations of painters.

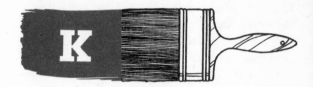

Kerosene is a petroleum distillate of relatively low volatility. It has an oily odor and leaves an oily residue. Used sparingly in hot weather, it can be used to slow the drying time of oil-based paints as you paint, which will help you have a better looking finish. Kerosene can also be used to soften cleaned brush bristles in a final bath before a brush is put back in its original keeper. It is important to use mineral spirits in a clean bath with a kerosene-soaked brush before painting with it again. This will remove traces of kerosene from your brush.

Kerosene is flammable and fire-prevention measures should be taken when using or storing it.

Ketone is an organic compound used in some thinners, paints and coatings.

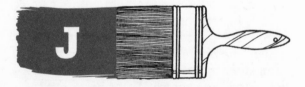

Journeyman: A person just learning the painting business is called an apprentice by the painting trade unions. A union painter who has completed a certain number of tests, both physical and written, and has usually four years' minimum

Knots: All wood knots should be sanded well and as much sap as possible removed before painting over them. To seal a wood knot when a pigmented paint is the finish, use first a shellac primer-sealer, a labeled knot sealer paint, or a stain-killer sealer in one or two coats.

This will prevent the knots from bleeding through. Two or three passes with a sealer on sappy wood such as pine may be needed to prevent bleeding through. However, some pine may require using a special pine-knot sealer paint for best results. Spackle or wood paste can be used to fill in wood knots but only after the knots have been sealed, so the sap deposits in the knots don't force the spackle or wood paste out in time. Aluminum paints can also be used to seal in wood knots, especially when a solid dark color is to be the finish paint coat, because aluminum paints are dark and deep in color.

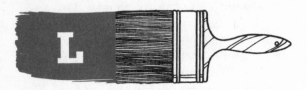

Lacquer is a nitrocellulose product that provides a quick-drying film finish that is impervious to water, mineral spirits, and alcohol. Its solvent is a special formulation, called lacquer thinner, that includes toluene, exylene, acetone, methyl-ethyl ketone, and other nasty-smelling stuff. Working with lacquer and lacquer thinners is both a health and an environmental hazard. Wear rubber gloves, eye protection and an organic vapor respirator (*see* **Masks**). Many areas require an approved spray booth for spraying lacquer. Lacquer is also highly flammable. Turn off pilot lights, use only sparkless fans, and be careful, even with light switches, when you're working with lacquer.

Clear lacquers are used on cabinets, furniture, and objects because of their durability and fast recoat time. I recommend using lacquer finishes on interior surfaces only. Don't apply lacquer over an old pigmented paint or varnish.

Because lacquer dries so fast, it is best sprayed. Lacquer doesn't sand very well, so the first coat on bare wood should be a special formulation called a lacquer sanding sealer. Lacquer stains and clear coatings tack up in five to twenty-five minutes. Some can be recoated in twenty to sixty minutes.

Brushing lacquers requires speed and skill to achieve a good finish. Don't use synthetic rollers or nylon brushes with lacquers, as they may disintegrate. Natural China bristle brushes work well.

Lacquer thinners can be used to thin certain oil-based paints to speed up their drying times. Lacquer thinners are recommended for cleaning up paint drips, spills, and overspray. They also work very well for cleaning up airless sprayer parts and spray tips. Don't thin lacquer-based stains or clear coatings with mineral spirits, as separation of the paint contents can occur. *See also* **Clear coatings** and **Refinishing.**

Ladder hangers are special wall-mounted hooks used for hanging an extension ladder horizontally when it is not in use. They can usually be purchased at big hardware stores.

Ladder jacks are clamplike devices that fasten to the rungs of two extension ladders so that a plank can be spread between them. Ladder jacks are necessary tools for most plank set-ups. Make sure when fastening them to a ladder that they are on good and tight! Also, be careful not to trip when climbing over them and onto the plank board. Ladder jacks can usually be purchased at large paint dealers and big hardware stores. They are usually made of steel or aluminum.

A **Ladder leg extension** fastens to the lower rails of an extension ladder and stabilizes it on uneven ground. Position the ladder straight up, then use your foot to lower the spring-loaded leg extension to the ground. With this device, pieces of wood or bricks and the like are not needed to level an extension ladder.

Ladders are very important tools, probably the largest in the painter's kit. Choose the right ladder for a particular job and use it safely. Most painters use one or two ladders: a stepladder (sometimes referred to as an A-frame) for indoor use and for heights up to 12 feet and an extension ladder for reaching greater heights, usually outdoors. There are also three-in-one and five-in-one all-purpose ladders that have come on the market recently. But these ladders are expensive, heavy, and awkward to use.

Metal ladders, of aluminum or magnesium, usually cost more than similar wooden ones. They are lighter and last longer than wooden ladders. Wooden ladders are bulky, heavy, and susceptible to weather and insect damage. They can also give you splinters. Fiberglass is the newest model ladder on the market, and it requires almost no upkeep or care. These ladders don't conduct electricity, like metal ones do; however, they cost more than metal or wooden ladders. Cable and telephone companies use them.

All new ladders should have a label on them that tells their duty rating, a figure that states the maximum weight they can sustain. A light-duty rating is around 175 to 200 pounds, medium-duty is around 200 to 250 pounds, and heavy-duty is around 250 pounds and up. Different ladder companies all have different duty ratings. Stepladders are also sometimes rated "household" and "commercial."

Stepladders come in 3-foot to 8-foot, 10-foot, and 12-foot, and even higher sizes. Step stools are smaller versions of stepladders and usually come in sizes of 2 feet or 3 feet. There are platform ladders, usually made of metal in 3-foot, 4-foot, and 5-foot

sizes, with hand safety rails and a big bucket-shelf space. These ladders are more comfortable to work on than stepladders, and even a 5-gallon container can rest on the bucket-shelf space.

Some extension ladders come in sizes of 12 feet, 16 feet, 20 feet, 24 feet, 28 feet, 32 feet, 36 feet, and 40 feet. Look for rubber traction on the rungs to prevent slipping on the extension ladder you are to buy or rent. Always make sure the ropes and pulleys work easily and that the extension pieces pull apart with little resistance.

Buy a stepladder a foot or more higher than what you think you will need it for. Buy an extension ladder at least 3 feet longer than the height you want to reach. Make sure before you buy a ladder that it comes with a warranty against defects.

Carry an extension ladder over your shoulder with both hands, or at waist-level, again with both hands. An extension ladder may be carried upright and "walked" by steadying the ladder with one hand securely gripping a rung, while the other hand lifts the ladder. Be sure to hold the ladder close or next to your shoulder. Balance and some muscle power make this carrying method possible, but don't attempt this method by yourself if the ladder is too long or heavy.

Never attempt to raise up from the ground by yourself an extension ladder of 32 feet or higher. One method of raising an extension ladder up from the ground is to put one side of the ladder firmly against a building and then walk toward the building, raising and reaching rung over rung on the ladder as it starts to straighten up. This method can also be used with one person holding one end of the ladder firmly in place with his feet while the ladder is walked and raised by another person. Always make sure the movable extension section and the side you'll be climbing is facing the ground before raising the ladder.

To avoid an extension ladder scraping or making scuff marks on a finish-paint

The best way to carry an extension ladder is by "walking" it to its destination. It takes muscle power and shouldn't be attempted alone if the ladder is very long or heavy.

coated surface, pad the top rails with clean rags, towels, or socks. Or use a ladder spreader.

Make sure your ladder is on firm, level, non-slippery ground. If you must use a ladder on unstable ground, be extra careful and consider tying it down or putting wooden blocks or a piece of plywood under it. On uneven ground, blocks of wood or bricks can also be used to level out a ladder. Or consider digging away the ground from under one leg. You can also use a ladder leg extension.

Always make sure before climbing a stepladder that the spreader braces are extended completely out and level. Make sure also on a stepladder that the bucket shelf is completely down and out. Before climbing up an extension ladder make sure the ladder hook locks are secure and won't slip out.

If the rope and pully parts of an extension ladder become stuck or won't work, try to fix them with the ladder lying flat on the ground. If that doesn't work, you may have to put the ladder back upright and then work off a stepladder and pull the movable section out by hand and push it up to the higher rung you desire it on.

Don't lean back too far on an extension ladder or reach out too far to the sides either. Keep your belt buckle within the ladder rails. It's a good idea to hold the rung of an extension ladder with one hand while brushing or spraying with the other hand. Set up most of your extension ladder positions in a 75 degree angle. Have at least a 15 percent to 20 percent overlap with each section of an extension ladder. Hold the rungs of an extension ladder when climbing it, not the sides; climb up using only one rung at a time.

Avoid reaching out any farther than this for safety reasons when you are working on an extension ladder.

If you are frightened when working on or when climbing an extension ladder, remember that there were others before you who felt or still feel the same way. By being careful, cautious and taking it easy, in time your fears may dissipate.

Use a ladder-stabilizer bar or apparatus when using an extension ladder.

Don't climb farther up the rungs than this when using an extension ladder.

When on a ladder and painting in front of a door, consider locking the door or placing a full fiver by the door to avoid having someone inadvertently open it. Don't ever place or rest a ladder against a window pane! Never slide down a ladder and never have more than one person on the same ladder.

There are platform stands that the phone and utility companies use. These connect to an extension ladder's rungs and are for standing on. This way, a person doesn't have to stand on the rungs directly. These platform stands increase stability and reduce fatigue.

If a wooden ladder is to be painted, use a clear satin finish instead of a pigmented paint. This way, you can still see cracks if they develop. A wooden ladder, whether step or extension, should be stored off the ground and sheltered from weathering in a dry area to help it last longer.

A **Ladder spreader** or stabilizer is a device that fits onto the top two rungs of an extension ladder, widens the ladders' contact with the house, and includes rubber feet to keep from marring it. This device usually gains a foot or more of space between the ladder and the house or building. Paint buckets, cans, and other tools can easily be hung on a ladder spreader. It is much easier to work off an extension ladder when a spreader is attached to it. A ladder spreader also makes an extension ladder safer and prevents it from sliding or moving across and sliding down. Ladder companies and large paint and hardware stores may carry this device.

Lap marks are pronounced brush or roller marks with a hard edge. To minimize the frequency of lap marks when using enamels, clear finishes, or semi-transparent stains, maintain a wet edge, always working toward the previous wet edge. Avoid stopping in the middle of your work; instead always have a good place to square-up, such as at a completed section or at a corner. Thin and stir your paints when they become sticky. Lap marks are fairly non-existent on solid-body stains and water-based pigmented flat finishes.

Latex paints are water-based, don't penetrate quite as well as oil-based paints, dry faster, and are relatively odorless. Latex paints include interior and exterior paints (of all glosses), enamels, undercoaters, and stains. Latex itself is a rubbery substance, and in paint it is suspended in an emulsion. Latex is also used in combination with resins like acrylic and vinyl to create special paints. Some people call any kind of water-based paint a latex paint even if it is actually a 100 percent acrylic paint.

Rolling and brushing with flat latex paints can go fast, because maintaining a wet edge or worrying about lap marks is not a problem in most cases. Generally speaking, latex paints require little or no thinning at all.

Latex paints form relatively flexible films that can withstand changing conditions. *See also* **Paint.**

Laundry rooms are usually high-moisture areas. Treat a laundry room like a bathroom when painting it.

Leaching is the migration of substance from underneath a paint film through to the surface. You can see this as brownish spots or streaks on a freshly painted surface. Most leaching on exterior surfaces will go away after one winter's weather. If it doesn't, try applying an alcohol or bleach solution. If all else fails, go ahead and do what you probably should have done before painting: apply an appropriate undercoater or stain killer and repaint.

Lifting, a result of poor adhesion, occurs when you paint over an undercoater or first coat of paint that is not completely dry. The moisture of the new coat causes the first coat to lift or wrinkle. You may have to strip the paint off and start over again or sand off the paint. *See also* **Drying.**

Lighting is important for quality painting. Even before beginning to work, paint choice depends on lighting because colors look different under different lights: tungsten light bulbs are relatively orange, fluorescent light is green, and daylight (depending on the time of day) can be blue or red. Color samples, or "chips," should therefore be viewed in the same lighting conditions as they will be used. *See* **Color.**

When painting, avoid glare. The best light is daylight; supplement it with a mechanic's or trouble light, if necessary, to accent holidays and uneven brush or roller strokes.

Linseed oil is an amber to brown oil that is extracted from flax seed. It is the most frequently used oil in commercial paint because it is a relatively inexpensive drying oil. A drying oil will oxidize when exposed to air, forming a hard film.

There are two types of linseed oil available on the market: raw linseed oil, which dries very slowly, and boiled linseed oil, which is not really boiled but heat-treated and combined with heavy metal driers. Either one can be used in paint to slow drying time, the raw more than the boiled. Either one can also be used as a clear penetrating finish on its own. *See* **Drying** and **Oil finishes.**

Liquid sandpaper, the commonly used term for a liquid deglosser, is sold in paint and hardware stores and takes the gloss off shiny surfaces, providing more tooth for paint to adhere to. Liquid sandpaper is not a substitute for granular sandpaper when it comes to smoothing a rough or uneven surface.

Louvers are usually made of wood, sometimes metal, and they should be cleaned, prepped, and painted as is appropriate for those materials. The only complication with louvers is that they're intricate. Therefore, the most efficient way to paint them is to take them down, bring them to some out-of-the-way, dust-free area, and spray them. Use a good-quality enamel for your finish coats if you want an elegant look and durability. Thin your paint slightly. Remember to spray from all angles on both sides, and to move the shutters up and down to cover all areas. Two thin coats are better than one thick coat. Sometimes drips and runs may occur when too thick a spray coat is applied; catch these with a brush before they dry hard. It is a good idea to move louver slats somewhat after they have become tacky and before they dry out completely, so that they won't get stuck in place.

Brushing louvers can be a nightmare and often does not result in a quality look. However, if you do use a brush, begin on the back, so that paint drips can be corrected when you brush out the front. Also, consider taking the louvers off and painting them on top of sawhorses or blocks of wood.

Machinery: For finish paint coats on machines and industrial equipment, an industrial-grade enamel, or a rust-resis-

tant enamel, in high gloss (some paint manufacturers will call it gloss) is recommended. The prep work on machinery generally consists of sanding, removing grease and oils with a degreaser, or using a T.S.P. (trisodium phosphate) and water solution for mild cleaning. All rust spots should be chipped and sanded and two coats of a rust-resistant primer applied. Any bare metal should be treated with a metal undercoater. Depending on the size of the machinery and the practicality of the circumstances, spray-painting, rolling, and brushing are all good ways to go. A fast-drying stain-killer can be used on scuff marks and other spots to prevent bleed-through.

Maintenance-painting is the painting of buildings at a stage when they require only minor prep work and one coat of paint, instead of waiting longer and having a major prep job on your hands. Maintenance-painting is cost-effective. Hospitals, public schools, the military, the government, property managers, and smart people everywhere know the value of maintenance-painting.

The average exterior usually needs repainting every four to six years, longer on a northern exposure because there's less sunlight, which can shorten the lifespan of a paint job. A building will weather fastest on southern and western exposures. The average interior gets repainted every five to seven years, but this is more a matter of personal preference than of maintenance.

Consider repainting when you notice that colors have faded, the gloss on enamels is dull, chalking is starting, checking or small cracks are occurring, or bare wood or metal is just starting to show from underneath a paint coat.

Marbleizing is creating the look of marble using paint, usually on a wood surface. It is not antiquing or glazing. Begin by preparing the surface, sanding it smooth, and filling any holes or cracks. Next, apply three or four coats of special tinted enamel to the surface, sanding between coats. Then apply shellac, and when it dries, rub it with fine steel wool. Then apply kerosene and a glaze. While the glaze is still wet, use a brush, a sponge, and sometimes a feather to achieve the final look. The trick is to understand what marble looks like in the first place. There are books available that deal exclusively with marbleizing and other faux finishes. Also, an experienced painter or a paint-store owner or manager may be able to help you. It is a good idea to experiment on scrap pieces before marbleizing where people will see it.

Marine enamels and varnishes are specially formulated for durability in harsh marine environments. Generally they are more flexible than other paints and varnishes and more resistant to moisture and corrosive elements. *See also* **Enamels, Spar varnish, Clear coatings,** and **Varnishes.**

Masking machines are used mostly for spray-painting jobs. They dispense bigger pieces of tape and masking paper than you can with a hand-masking machine. Roll sizes are usually 18 inches to 36 inches wide and 100 feet long. Blade sizes are usually either 18 inches or 36 inches wide. If you do a lot of spray painting, a masking machine is a necessity. *See* **Hand-masking machine.**

Masking tape is handy to have on most painting jobs. When spraying, it is a must. Use it to block off areas or to create straight cut-in lines (uniform lines on a wall) or separate blocks of colors on walls. It covers baseboards, protects hardware, and helps build makeshift spray booths. Use masking tape in conjunction with plastic bags or sheeting to protect objects, such as door knobs, vents, or hung fixtures that aren't going to be removed before painting. Don't put masking tape on wallpaper; it can tear the paper when it's removed. If masking tape is used on bare metal surfaces or window glass, remove it as soon as possible, especially when it's used in direct sunlight, because it will leave a sticky residue. Use mineral spirits to remove this. Blue masking tapes that don't leave a sticky residue are available, but they cost much more than ordinary masking tape.

To remove masking tape that's been painted over, wait until the paint is fully dry and slice along the cut-in line with a razor blade. This way, when you peel off the tape, the paint film edge will not crack off with it.

Masks: Particle masks are designed for keeping dust, paint chips, and sanding particles from your respiratory system. They consist of a paperlike filtering material, held over your nose and mouth by a piece of elastic. They are inexpensive, only a little uncomfortable (you can get sweaty behind them), and a good idea whenever you're doing any prep work or clean-up, including sweeping, that raises dust. Dust can build up in your lungs over years, so it's important to remember to use protection.

Particle masks are not the same as organic vapor respirators, which are essential when spraying paints. These are more elaborate than the filter masks because they place a rubber seal against your face and have replaceable charcoal filters that not only block particles but also absorb harmful volatile compounds. Paint overspray and solvent fumes are threats to your health. Use protection and change your charcoal filter whenever you begin to smell odors.

Remember, too, that masks and respirators are to be used in addition to adequate ventilation.

Masonry includes stonework, brick, stucco, cement, and concrete. All these are subject to efflorescence (sometimes called salting or chalking), which is the formation of alkali mineral deposits on the surface. Do not paint over alkali. Remove it with an acid solution (*see* **Muriatic acid**), scrape off any peeled paint, and seal the surface with a masonry conditioner. Then apply a finish paint labeled alkali-resistant. Most of the flat paints used on masonry surfaces are water-based latex, acrylic, or vinyl. These work better on masonry surfaces than similar oil-based paints.

If there is no evidence of efflorescence, you may get away with using only alkali-resistant paint and no conditioner. Rough masonry surfaces should be sprayed with an airless sprayer, rolled with a long-nap roller cover, or both together; these painting methods force the paint into all the crevices.

Water problems on masonry surfaces can usually be traced to improper grading, a blocked drainage pipe, leaky gutters, a misrouted downspout, or water leaking through the floor plates. It's best first to correct the source of the problem. Then, after the surface is completely dry, use a masonry waterproofing paint to seal it. Don't apply a masonry waterproofing paint if the surface or air temperature is below 55 degrees Fahrenheit. *See also* **Basements** and **Paint.**

Masonry conditioner is a thin, oil-based primer that penetrates masonry surfaces and seals against efflorescence on the masonry surface. Masonry conditioners are quick and easy to apply. They should be stirred well and often during use. Don't use a masonry conditioner on anything except masonry surfaces.

Unless a specific masonry conditioner says differently on its label, wait seventy-two to eighty-four hours before recoating for best results.

Matte refers to a dull, low-gloss surface. Certain clear coatings and enamels have matte finishes.

Metals: New metal surfaces should be cleaned with thinners such as naphtha , mineral spirits, lacquer thinner, or turpentine to get rid of any oil, grease, or dust before priming with a metal undercoater. These solvents also help create a better bond for paint. Some metals exposed to and affected by salt air can be cleaned with a warm-water and detergent solution, but don't use water on ferrous metals because they will rust. New or bare aluminum should be etched before painting. *See* **Etching**.

Most metals exposed to air for any length of time will evidence oxidation, which should be removed before painting. Oxidation on some metals can be cleaned by using lemon juice, salt, and elbow grease. Stronger acids work to etch metal, as well as to clean it. Ferrous metals require scraping, sanding, or more vigorous means to remove rust. Once a ferrous metal surface has been cleaned, it should be primed with rust-resistant or red-lead primer as soon as possible, because rust can form quickly. Some metal surfaces require specific kinds of metal undercoaters for best results. Check the label of your undercoater.

Metal undercoaters and finish paints used over metal surfaces should be applied as thickly as possible for added protection. Brushing or rolling undercoaters on metal surfaces is recommended over spraying because the undercoater should be worked into the surface. Spray metal undercoater only if someone is following you to work the wet paint into the surface by brushing or rolling it. Finish coats, however, can be sprayed on if desired.

Some spray paints combine a metal primer and finish paint in one can, and they can be used on some metal surfaces. These should be used only for interior metals, where there is little or no corrosion. On larger metal areas, spray cans are not cost-effective or as thorough as brushing, rolling or airless spray-painting.

Metal surface fillers, available at some paint stores, can be used for filling pores and pits in metals. Little or no shrinking occurs with these fillers, so one pass, leveling the filler flush, usually suffices.

Most metals are finish-enameled for durability. An industrial enamel or a rust-fighting enamel are good choices. Two or three finish coats are recommended. Semi-gloss and high-gloss sheens generally look better and give better protection than matte or satin glosses.

Clear coatings and stains are not recommended for metal surfaces because they provide little protection and will deteriorate rapidly, and then they will have to be stripped. *See also* **Galvanized** and **Paint.**

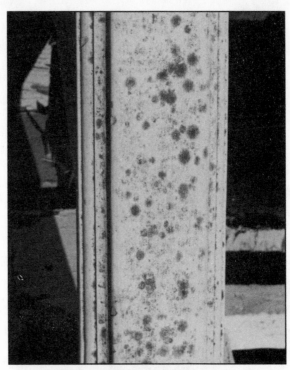

Mildew shown here is in full bloom on door trim. It must be removed completely before painting.

When painting metal railings, any one of these tools works well with a brush. From the left: railing roller, toilet roller, and painter's mitt.

Mildew is a green or black fungus commonly found on wood surfaces and masonry where there is little sunlight and much dampness. Mildew must be eliminated completely before an undercoater or finish-paint coat is applied. Untreated mildew will grow through paint and can become an even worse problem.

Fortunately, mildew can be killed fairly easily with common household bleach. For severe cases spray on bleach at full strength or at four parts bleach to one part water. T.S.P. (trisodium phosphate) improves the wetting properties of bleach and water. One of the best ways to apply bleach is with a garden pump-action portable sprayer. Wear goggles and protect your face and skin. Don't spray bleach through a paint sprayer, as it can ruin the gun. Let the bleach sit for a while. As the bleach kills the mildew, the mildew will change to a yellow color and fade. When this occurs, rinse the area thoroughly with water. Use a fast-drying stain killer for added protection before painting.

You can also add a mildew retardant, or mildewcide, to your paint. Have it added and mixed by your paint dealer.

To get rid of mildew, use a garden pump sprayer and spray bleach from it directly onto the mildew.

But if you add mildew retardant yourself, stir it in thoroughly, and don't let it contact your skin. Put mildew retardants in any finish paint that is going where there's dampness or little sunlight.

Sometimes yellowish flash spots can occur on paint coats that have mildew retardants added to them, but these should go away in a few days or weeks. If not, put another coat of paint over them.

If possible, find and correct the cause of the dampness that's causing the mildew. Cracks and holes in a surface, or sweaty or leaky pipes can be the culprit. *See also* **Prep-work.**

Mill scale is a loosely used term for any combination of rust, dirt, grease, grime, soot, or oil that forms on a metal surface. Mill scale must be removed before an undercoater or finish paint coat is applied. *See also* **Metals** and **Rust.**

Mineral spirits is a petroleum distillate for thinning oil-based paint. It comes in various grades: heavy for slower drying, light for faster drying. Mineral spirits can clean oil deposits and greasy residues from metal and other surfaces. It rids surfaces of paint-remover residue that occurs after stripping. And, of course, it's ideal for cleaning brushes and rollers used with oil-based paints. *See* **Clean-up.**

For economy, buy mineral spirits in the largest quantity you can. It doesn't go bad, and it's always good to have plenty on hand for clean-up.

Mitt: A painter's mitt, which somewhat resembles a baseball glove, is usually made of sheepskin or a synthetic equivalent, the same materials used for roller covers. Mitts come in different sizes and textures and fit your hand. you put the mitt on, dip it into the paint, and then wipe it on the surface to be painted. Mitts are useful for painting heating and ventilating ducts, pipes, gutters, light poles, railings, machinery, and even furniture. Have a brush or a 3-inch roller set-up handy to even things out and catch drips when you're working with a mitt. Painter's mitts hold a good amount of paint and can increase your speed on odd-shaped objects, but they are messy. Be sure to lay down sufficient drop cloths when using them.

Moisture: Paints and moisture are natural enemies. Nothing causes paint problems more than moisture, whether the detrimental effect be cracking, alligatoring, checking, mildew, or peeling. Because reasons for such problems can vary from house to house and climate to climate, identifying the specific cause is a job that should be handled locally. Therefore, whenever you are in doubt as to the proper solution for unusual weathering outside your house or a chronic moisture problem inside, consult the manager of your paint store. What follows are some general solutions.

To alleviate moisture problems outside, fix leaky gutters and pipes and use undercoaters on all trim work, followed by two or more coats of semi-gloss or high-gloss enamels. Marine enamels are excellent choices for trim work. It is debatable as to what is better for fighting moisture problems: oil-based or water-based enamels. Many argue that latex or acrylic enamels allow more movement, that moisture doesn't get under them as easily, and that bubbling is not as much a problem with them as with oil-based paints. Others argue that oil-based films are more difficult for water to penetrate. I use the top-of-the-line water-based enamels whenever I can because (in my opinion) they are just as good as oil-based paints and I don't like the fumes associated with the latter.

To prevent moisture inside, the following should be done: Install vents in kitchens and bathrooms. Open bathroom windows and doors after your shower. Make sure attics and crawl spaces are properly vented. Fix leaky pipes. Caulk or patch cracks and holes in surfaces outside and inside the house. If all else fails, consider installing small louvers directly in your siding to vent moisture trapped in the walls. If your basement walls leak, determine the cause and fix it. If your basement floor is dirt, install a plastic vapor barrier or lay down some concrete. *See also* **Ventilation, Mildew,** and **Prep work.**

Moulding: *See* **Trim.**

Mullions and **Muntins** are part of the window sash. They are the vertical and horizontal members that divide the panes of a window.

Muriatic acid is another name for hydrochloric acid. It can be used in a 6 percent to 10 percent solution with water for treating efflorescence on masonry surfaces. For etching or putting tooth on slick, glossy floors, a solution of one part muriatic acid with two or three parts water should do the job.

Always wear goggles, protective clothing, and acid-resisting gloves, and use plastic or glass containers instead of metal ones when using muriatic acid. Remember to pour the muriatic acid into the water and not the water into the muriatic acid to prevent the water from boiling and splattering onto your face or body.

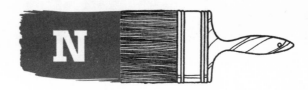

Naphtha is a colorless, flammable liquid obtained from coal tar and other materials. It is used as a thinner and a solvent. Some thinners that contain naphtha are fast-drying and can be used to speed up the drying times of most oil-based paints. After sanding custom work, use naphtha thinners on a clean rag to wipe down the surface prior to top-coating.

Non-skid paint additive is a gritty, sandy substance that can be added to paint, and when the paint dries, the result is a textured, non-skid surface. It works very well. Don't use your best brush for application, however, because it will be difficult to rinse.

Oak is an open-grained wood that may need a wood paste filler for a smooth surface. *See* **Woods**.

Odor: If you are particularly sensitive to odors, you should use water-based undercoaters and paints. Even then, good ventilation is essential. Don't use cheap paints that have an offensive odor (some people put vanilla extract in paint to disguise the odor). Consider using an odorless thinner with your oil-based paints. Some paint stores even carry paint fragrance additives that could solve your problem.

Odorless thinners are usually more costly than regular mineral spirits and can be used only with certain oil-based paints.

Oil-based paints are known for their penetration and durability. *See* **Enamels** and **Paint**.

Oil finishes consist of what are sometimes called rubbing oils or penetrating oils. Linseed oil, tung oil, and blends of these and other finishing oils are distinguished from, say, cooking oils in that they dry. Many oils will thicken with evaporation, but only a few will dry hard. Finishing oils dry hard because of a reaction with oxygen called polymerization. Depending on the oil, this can take some time. Finishing oils therefore can penetrate into a porous wood surface and harden within that surface. This protects and beautifies the wood without creating a film on top of it.

But finishing oils do not protect wood surfaces as well as film finishes (like clear coatings and paints) do. Therefore use an oil finish where you do not need sturdy protection from dirt, water, moisture, or the elements; use an oil finish on interior surfaces, especially fine furniture and cabinets.

Without going to extremes, the more times a rubbing oil is applied, the better a finish becomes. Warming a rubbing oil before applying decreases its viscosity and therefore increases its penetration, at least for the first coat. Once the first coat begins to harden in the wood, subsequent coats build on that and do not penetrate any deeper. Let each oil coat dry for at least a day. After several coats, let the surface cure for a couple of weeks. Then you can adjust the sheen of your oil finish by rubbing with a mild abrasive, like pumice or rottenstone, mixed with some mineral oil. Rub it off with a clean soft cloth.

Mineral oil is the main ingredient in most furniture polishes. Mineral oil is a non-drying oil, and as such, aids in dust removal and gives a temporary shine to furniture. Mineral oil is often scented, which adds to its appeal. *See also* **Refinishing**.

Outdoor furniture: Here's a plan for painting your outdoor furniture: First, take all the pillows and cushions off the outside furniture and put them out of your way. Look over the furniture and correct any loose parts, bolts, nails, and so forth. Lay some drops out and put all the furniture on them. Next, do all the chipping, scraping, sanding, caulking, patching, and necessary undercoating. After the undercoater has dried completely, construct a temporary spray booth out of plastic sheeting, using a staple gun and masking tape, making it big enough to move around in easily. Patio areas with beams or poles, or a garage, are good places to locate this booth. If your spray booth is large enough, spray all the furniture at one time. Spray two or three thin coats, instead of one thick one for best results. If it isn't large enough for all the furniture, rotate the furniture in and out as it is spray-finished. Industrial enamels, rust-resistant enamels, and marine enamels are good finishes to consider using for metal furniture. *See also* **Enamels** and **Marine enamels.** Stains work best on furniture that is bare or previously stained wood but not over a flat- or enamel-painted surface. *See* **Stains.**

Overhangs, or eaves, can be cleaned by waterblasting, using garden hoses, brooms, scrapers and sandpaper. Consider using a pole sander at least to scratch the surface, for a better bond.

Overhangs are prone to mildew, because the sun never shines there. Be careful when applying bleach to remove mildew overhead; protect your eyes with goggles. Also protect your face and skin; wash off any bleach that gets onto your skin.

The fastest way to paint overhangs is with an airless sprayer and a person with a roller and brush set-up following right behind to work the paint or undercoater into the surface. The next fastest method is to use a 9-inch roller set-up and a cut-in brush.

Oxidation: *See* **Rust.**

Pad applicators and edgers are square or rectangular foamlike devices with handles that come in many sizes. Most professional painters don't use these tools. However, if you find they work for you, then by all means use them.

Paint: Technically speaking, paint is a solid or liquid mixture of pigment, binder, and solvent, used to decorate and/or protect a surface. This definition includes flats, enamels, stains, clear finishes, primers, sealers, and undercoaters.

The most commonly used kinds of paints are oil-based and water-based. Oil-based paints are thinned with mineral spirits or turpentine, and they include all alkyds (which have largely replaced vegetable-oil-based paints) and most varnishes. Water-based paints are made from latex, acrylic, or vinyl resins and are thinned with water.

It used to be that oil-based paints were the only serious paint material, but water-based paints are improving all the time, and now there is a water-based alternative for just about every oil-based product. Meanwhile, with the introduction of alkyd and other synthetic resins, oil-based paints have improved, too. They're more durable and less odorous than they were. Oil-based paints are preferred for their penetration, durability, and compatibility (they'll cover most other finishes). Water-based paints are preferred for being easy to use and clean up after, quick drying, and odor-free. They are also recommended on masonry surfaces and bare wallboard. Quality oil- and water-based paints are both good and durable, and it is debatable which is better than the other. *See* **Alkyd, Enamel, Latex,** and **Thinners.**

Paints are designated "exterior," "interior," or "exterior/interior." Interior paints are generally less toxic than similar exterior paints, they are also usually smoother, and many of them take tints better than exterior paints. But they will not stand up to weather. You can use an exterior paint indoors, but don't use an interior paint outdoors. An exterior/interior paint can be used inside or outside.

The main thing to remember about paints is: You get what you pay for. For best results, always buy the top-of-the-line paints of a particular paint manufacturer. Generally speaking, these have more solids, which means better coverage, more consistent, longer-lasting color, and a more durable film. Many times two coats of economy paints are needed to cover the way one coat of a premium paint can. Don't try and stretch any paints by over-thinning. Old or previously frozen paints that smell bad or are curdled or lumpy should be thrown away. If a paint has begun to skin over, its quality is compromised. If the skin on an almost-full gallon or fiver of paint is not too thick, however, the paint can still be used without concern.

In the painting world, materials generally account for only 10 percent to 25 percent of the costs; labor is the expensive part of most jobs. So, if you're doing the job yourself, why skimp and use a cheap, inferior material? Always do quality work with quality materials, and you'll be happy with the job for a long time.

Drying time, recoat time, and coverage varies, depending on type of paint, type of surface, and atmospheric conditions. Below is a chart that gives some guidelines. However, it is not meant as a substitute for the label on your can of paint. Don't ignore paint labels!

#	PAINT	DRYING TIME	RECOAT TIME	COVERAGE (SQ. FT/GAL)
1.	Interior, water-based latex or vinyl-acrylic (wall sealer)	2-3 hours	4-6 hours	375-475
2.	Interior, oil-based (wall primer-sealer)	4-5 hours	13-18 hours	325-425
3.	Interior, water-based, latex, flat (ceilings and walls)	30-90 minutes	5-6 hours	325-425
4.	Interior, oil-based (wood stain)	10-18 hours	24-36 hours	175-575
5.	Interior, lacquer, (clear)	10-30 minutes	30-60 minutes	225-275
6.	Interior, lacquer, (wood stains)	15-30 minutes	30-60 minutes	275-475
7.	Interior, oil-based, varnish (clear)	2-3 hours	12-18 hours	475-575
8.	Interior, oil-based, polyurethane (clear)	1½-3 hours	8-12 hours	375-575
9.	Interior, oil-based, varnish (floor)	2-5 hours	5-10 hours	475-675
10.	Interior, water-based, flat (acoustic ceiling)	45-90 minutes	4-6 hours	80-275
11.	Interior, water-based (commercial ceiling)	45-90 minutes	13-18 hours	75-175
12.	Exterior, interior, oil-based, alkyd (semi-gloss enamel)	4-6 hours	24-36 hours	325-425
13.	Exterior, interior, epoxy, ready-made or two-component (enamel)	8-12 hours	15-24 hours	325-375
14.	Exterior, interior, water-based, acrylic (all-purpose undercoater)	45-90 minutes	4-6 hours	325-475
15.	Exterior, interior, oil-based, alkyd (enamel/undercoater)	15-24 hours	24-36 hours	375-475
16.	Exterior, interior, water-based, latex or acrylic, (wood undercoater)	35-90 minutes	7-9 hours	325-425
17.	Exterior, interior, oil-based, alkyd (wood undercoater)	13-17 hours	30-50 hours	275-475
18.	Exterior, interior, water-based, acrylic (flat)	35-60 minutes	6-8 hours	325-425

#	PAINT	DRYING TIME	RECOAT TIME	COVERAGE (SQ. FT/GAL)
19.	Exterior, interior, water-based, latex, vinyl-acrylic (flat)	2-3 hours	12-15 hours	250-400
20.	Exterior, interior, water-based, acrylic (enamel)	1½-3 hours	12-18 hours	375-475
21.	Exterior, interior, water-based, latex (enamel)	5-8 hours	18-24 hours	200-400
22.	Exterior, interior, oil-based (high-gloss enamel)	12-18 hours	25-50 hours	375-475
23.	Exterior, interior, water-based, acrylic (metal primer)	35-90 minutes	3-5 hours	325-375
24.	Exterior, interior, oil-based (metal primer)	3-8 hours	25-36 hours	325-375
25.	Exterior, interior, oil-based (rust primer)	12-18 hours	24-36 hours	375-575
26.	Exterior, interior, water-based, latex (solid-body stain)	1-3 hours	6-9 hours	90-340
27.	Exterior, interior, oil-based (semi-transparent stain)	6-10 hours	25-50 hours	90-325
28.	Exterior, interior, oil-based (industrial enamel)	3-7 hours	12-24 hours	325-375
29.	Exterior, interior, oil-based (rust-fighting enamel)	7-15 hours	13-18 hours	325-375
30.	Exterior, interior, oil-based (stain-killer/sealer)	30-50 minutes	90-120 minutes	250-390
31.	Exterior, interior, shellac (primer/sealer)	30-45 minutes	45-90 minutes	200-325
32.	Exterior, interior, water-based, pigmented, acrylic-latex (porch and floor)	1½-3 hours	15-20 hours	275-375
33.	Exterior, interior, liquid plastic (clear high gloss)	4-7 hours	10-12 hours	390-470
34.	Exterior, interior, oil-based (industrial floor enamel)	48-60 hours	65-72 hours	190-290
35.	Exterior, interior, oil-based (marine spar varnish)	13-26 hours	25-50 hours	475-575
36.	Exterior, interior, oil-based (wood preservative)	24-48 hours	50-60 hours	140-190
37.	Exterior, interior, oil-based (masonry conditioner)	12-20 hours	48-84 hours	175-275
38.	Exterior, interior, water-based acrylic, (block filler)	2-4 hours	12-18 hours	60-90
39.	Exterior, interior, silicone (clear water repellent)	1½-3 hours	50-75 hours	40-120
40.	Interior (sanding sealer)	15-45 minutes	2-3 hours	No specs given
41.	Exterior, interior, oil-based, red-oxide (rust primer)	8-12 hours	12-18 hours	375-575
42.	Exterior, interior, zinc chromate (metal primer)	4-6 hours	12-18 hours	300-375
43.	Exterior, interior, oil-based (enamel spray-can)	1-4 hours	5-9 hours	20-30

KINDS OF AREAS OR SURFACES	SUGGESTED PAINTS AND UNDERCOATERS TO USE
Acoustic (ceilings)	3, 10, 11, 12, 14, 18, 19, 20, 21, 22, 28, 30 31
Aluminum	3, 12, 13, 18, 19, 20, 21, 22, 23, 24, 25, 28, 29, 30, 41, 42, 43
Banisters	4, 5, 6, 7, 8, 12, 13, 14, 15, 16, 17, 20, 21, 22, 27 28, 30, 31, 33, 35, 36, 43
Baseboards	4, 5, 6, 7, 8, 12, 13, 14, 15, 16, 17, 20, 21, 22, 26, 27, 28, 30, 31, 33, 35, 36
Basement	1, 2, 3, 12, 13, 14, 18, 19, 20, 21, 22, 28, 30, 31, 37, 38, 39
Bathroom	1, 2, 12, 13, 14, 15, 16, 17, 20, 21, 22, 28, 30, 31
Bathtub	See **Porcelain.**
Block (walls)	12, 13, 14, 18, 19, 20, 21, 22, 28, 30, 31, 37, 38
Boats	35; use only specifically labeled and formulated boat or marine paints
Brass	22, 23, 24, 25, 28, 29, 30, 33, 35, 42
Bricks	3, 8, 12, 13, 14, 18, 19, 20, 21, 22, 28, 30, 33, 35, 37, 38, 39
Cabinets (wood)	4, 5, 6, 7, 8, 12, 13, 14, 15, 16, 17, 20, 21, 22, 27, 28, 30, 33, 35, 36, 40
Cars	Use only specifically labeled and formulated car paints.
Ceilings (beamed)	4, 5, 6, 7, 8, 12, 13, 14, 15, 16, 17, 18, 19, 20, 21, 22, 26, 27, 28, 30, 33, 35, 36, 39, 40
Ceilings (interior)	1, 2, 3, 11, 12, 13, 14, 15, 18, 19, 20, 21, 22, 28, 30, 31, 37
Chimneys	12, 13, 14, 18, 19, 20, 21, 22, 28, 30, 37
Cinder block	12, 13, 14, 18, 19, 20, 21, 22, 28, 30, 37, 38
Closets (drywall or plaster)	See Drywall or Plaster in this section.
Columns	12, 13, 14, 18, 19, 20, 21, 22, 28, 30, 37, 38
Concrete	12, 13, 14, 18, 19, 20, 21, 22, 28, 30, 32, 34, 37, 38, 39
Corbels	12, 14, 15, 16, 17, 18, 19, 20, 21, 22, 26, 27, 28, 30, 36, 39
Corridors	12, 13, 14, 18, 19, 20, 21, 22, 28, 30, 37, 38, 39
Decks & porches (wooden)	12, 13, 14, 15, 16, 17, 20, 21, 22, 26, 27, 28, 32, 33, 34, 35, 36, 39
Decks (concrete)	13, 30, 32, 34, 37, 39
Dormers (wooden)	12, 14, 15, 16, 17, 18, 19, 20, 21, 22, 26, 27, 28, 30, 36, 39
Downspouts & gutters (metal)	12, 13, 14, 20, 21, 22, 23, 24, 25, 28, 29, 30, 41, 42
Drawers (wooden)	4, 5, 6, 7, 8, 12, 13, 14, 15, 16, 17, 20, 21, 22, 27, 28, 30, 33, 35, 36, 39, 40, 43
Dressers (wooden)	4, 5, 6, 7, 8, 12, 13, 14, 15, 16, 17, 20, 21, 22, 27, 28, 30, 33, 35, 36, 39, 40, 43
Drywall	1, 2, 3, 12, 14, 18, 19, 20, 21, 22, 28, 30, 31
Duct & vent fixtures	12, 13, 14, 18, 19, 20, 21, 22, 23, 24, 25, 28, 29, 30, 41, 42, 43
Eaves (wooden)	12, 14, 16, 17, 18, 19, 20, 21, 22, 26, 27, 28, 30, 36, 39
Fascia board	12, 13, 14, 15, 16, 17, 20, 21, 22, 28, 30, 36, 39
Fences (wooden)	12, 14, 15, 16, 17, 18, 19, 20, 21, 22, 26, 27, 28, 30, 36, 39
Fences (metal)	12, 14, 20, 21, 22, 23, 24, 25, 28, 30, 41, 42, 43
Fiberboard	5, 7, 8, 12, 14, 16, 17, 18, 19, 20, 21, 22, 26, 28, 30, 33, 35, 36, 39

KINDS OF AREAS OR SURFACES	SUGGESTED PAINTS AND UNDERCOATERS TO USE
Flagpole	12, 13, 14, 20, 21, 22, 23, 24, 25, 28, 29, 30, 41, 42, 43
Flashing (metal)	12, 14, 18, 19, 20, 21, 22, 23, 24, 25, 28, 29, 30, 41, 42
Floor (concrete)	13, 30, 32, 34, 37
Floor (wooden)	4, 8, 9, 16, 17, 27, 30, 33, 34, 35, 36, 39
Furniture (interior, refinishing)	4, 5, 6, 7, 8, 27, 33, 35, 36, 40
Furniture (wood, for outdoor use)	13, 16, 17, 22, 27, 28, 30, 33, 35, 36, 39, 43
Furniture (metal)	See Metals in this section.
Gable	See either Metals or Woods in this section.
Handrails (metal)	12, 13, 22, 23, 24, 25, 28, 29, 30, 41, 42, 43
Heater (wall)	12, 13, 22, 23, 24, 25, 28, 29, 30, 41, 42, 43
House (exterior)	See Metals, Masonry, and Woods in this section.
House (interior)	See Metals, Masonry, Drywall, and Woods in this section.
Industrial (metal)	23, 24, 25, 28, 29, 30, 41, 42
Industrial (wood)	16, 17, 28, 30, 36, 39
Laundry room	12, 13, 14, 15, 22, 28, 30
Louvers (wood)	4, 5, 6, 7, 8, 12, 13, 14, 15, 16, 17, 20, 22, 27, 28, 30, 33, 35, 36, 43
Machinery	See Industrial (metal) in this section.
Masonry	12, 14, 18, 19, 20, 21, 22, 28, 30, 37, 38, 39
Metals (ferrous)	12, 13, 18, 19, 20, 21, 22, 23, 24, 25, 28, 29, 30, 41, 42
Overhangs & underhangs	12, 14, 15, 16, 17, 18, 19, 20, 21, 22, 26, 27, 28, 30, 35, 36, 39
Paneling (clear or stained finish)	See Refinishing in this section.
Pillars	See Columns in this section.
Pipes (exposed)	12, 13, 14, 18, 19, 20, 21, 22, 23, 24, 25, 28, 29, 30, 41, 42
Pipes (underground)	Use coal-tar enamels.
Plaster (interior)	3, 12, 13, 14, 18, 19, 20, 21, 22, 28, 30, 37, 38, 39
Plaster (exterior)	See Stucco in this section.
Plastic & rubber	13, or use specifically labeled paints and undercoaters for plastic or rubber surfaces.
Plywood	See **Plywood** & various surfaces.
Poles (metal)	See Flagpole in this section.
Refinishing (interior wood)	4, 5, 6, 7, 8, 33, 35, 40
Refrigerator	See **Porcelain.**
Screens	See **Screens.**
Shingle & shake roofs (wood)	16, 17, 18, 19, 22, 26, 27, 28, 30, 36, 39

KINDS OF AREAS OR SURFACES	SUGGESTED PAINTS AND UNDERCOATERS TO USE
Shutters (wood)	12, 14, 15, 16, 17, 20, 21, 22, 28, 30, 39
Siding (wood)	12, 14, 15, 16, 17, 18, 19, 20, 21, 22, 26, 27, 28, 30, 33, 35, 36, 39
Sinks & stoves	See **Porcelain.**
Stairs & steps (wood)	12, 13, 14, 16, 17, 20, 21, 22, 26, 27, 28, 30, 32, 33, 34, 35, 36, 39
Stones	See Masonry in this section.
Stucco	12, 14, 18, 19, 20, 22, 28, 30, 37, 39
Tiles (unglazed)	13, or specifically labeled tile paints
Traffic	See Traffic paints under **Paint.**
Trellis (wood)	12, 16, 17, 18, 19, 20, 21, 22, 26, 28, 30, 36, 39, 43
Trim (exterior or wood)	12, 14, 16, 17, 20, 21, 22, 28, 30, 33, 35, 36, 39
Trim (interior or wood)	4, 5, 6, 7, 8, 12, 14, 15, 16, 17, 20, 21, 22, 27, 28, 30, 33, 35, 36, 40
Trim (metal)	See Metal in this section.
Windows (interior, wood)	See Trim, interior or wood, in this section.
Windows (interior, metal)	See Metals, ferrous, in this section.
Woods (interior, pigmented finish, colored-up)	4, 6, 12, 14, 15, 16, 17, 18, 19, 20, 21, 22, 26, 27, 28, 30
Woods (exterior, pigmented finish, colored-up)	12, 14, 15, 16, 17, 18, 19, 20, 21, 22, 26, 27, 28, 30
Woods (interior, clear finish)	5, 7, 33, 35, 36, 39, 40
Woods (exterior, clear finish)	33, 35, 36, 39

Painting as a profession: To achieve skill as a professional painter takes experience, understanding, and practice. Don't get frustrated, be patient, try to think positively, and don't ever say, "I can't do this." Approach your work with a quality attitude, use quality products, and leave the place with a feeling of pride.

A painting job should be looked at and sold as a long-term investment. Everybody benefits from a quality painting job, including the neighbors. A new coat of paint can increase the value of a home by at least 10 percent, making it more saleable, too.

The best way to begin in this profession is to work for someone else. Several different contractors, over a period of two to four years, will give you valuable experience. Once you are considered a professional painter, have some business cards printed up. Don't just say on your cards "Joe Doe the painter;" make them distinctive and make them represent the kind of work you do. This may be the only impression people have of you.

Hand out these cards to everybody and his brother. Over a period of a year or so you will be surprised at how many people have kept your card and call you for an estimate. Hand out your business cards, especially in areas where you are working or have just completed a job.

Your best source of business is referral, so leave your customers happy. Also remember: rooms, houses, everything that's painted requires repainting periodically, so look forward to repeat business.

Get letters of recommendation and take pictures of your work when you're first starting out. Keep records. Stay on top of your business. Don't underestimate the force of persistence, and in time you will have a successful business with your own clientele. *See also* **Appearances, Bids, Warranties,** and **Guarantees.**

Paint remover: The active ingredient in most paint removers (also called strippers) is methylene chloride, which is highly toxic to breathe and moderately toxic by skin contact. It can burn skin and eyes. Protect your eyes with goggles, wear rubber gloves, and work in a ventilated area, if not outside, when you're stripping paint. But don't work in direct sun. Methylene chloride is volatile. Most paint removers include a wax that forms a skin over the chemical to slow its evaporation. Therefore apply a paint remover with a minimum of brush strokes; the more you move it around, the more you interrupt the wax film and allow the methylene chloride to evaporate.

The more methylene chloride, the better. You can pretty much choose your stripper by weight: the heavier the can, the more potent. Deciding on a liquid versus a paste remover is a matter of application: The liquid makes sense for intricate surfaces that are horizontal; the paste won't run as much on flat, vertical surfaces.

Before starting to do any stripping, remove any hardware. Protect the area around the item being stripped from dripping remover. Apply stripper with an old brush. Polyester, tynex, and nylon brushes can sometimes get eaten up when they are used to apply paint remover. Natural brushes shouldn't be destroyed by paint remover, but you probably won't want to paint with them afterwards. Apply the stripper as thick as possible, and let it do its work for the recommended time.

To remove the stripper, you can use a scraper for flat surfaces. Scrape lightly, or you'll damage the surface. Rags and paper towels work quite well, and for intricate surfaces, sawdust does a good job of absorbing stripper. You may want to use a toothbrush, wire brush (brass is softer than steel and won't scratch most hardwoods), or steel wool to work the paint or finish loose, but don't expect steel wool to absorb any stripper. Sanding is usually not necessary on surfaces that have been stripped. If they were sanded before a finish or paint was applied, there's nothing the stripper has done to unsand them. In fact, a piece of fine furniture can be ruined by sanding.

Rinse the surface with mineral spirits or denatured alcohol to clean up the paint-remover residue; otherwise the wax may inhibit the bonding of your paint or finish.

Some paint stores carry special liquid paint removers, which involve a three-step application. These big-job paint removers are an alternative to torching to remove paints; they're not very gentle, but because they don't scorch the wood, they can be used to prepare surfaces for a clear finish. They also work on large, rough surfaces, such as decks and siding. Always read the label completely before using such products.

Commercial stripping operations are not recommended for furniture you care about, especially antiques. The furniture is dipped in stripper and hosed off. That much moisture wreaks havoc on furniture joints.

Paneling: If an enamel or flat finish is desired as a finish-paint coat on unpainted or bare wood paneling, the wood paneling should first be cleaned and sanded and then a good wood undercoater applied. Two coats of a wood undercoater are sometimes needed for best results. Two finish coats of a flat or enamel paint are recommended.

Bare, unpainted, or stained wood paneling can be clear-coated with either clear lacquers, varnishes, polyurethanes, or oil.

Make sure you sand well, regardless of what finish goes on wood paneling, to put some tooth in the surface.

Particleboard and other man-made panels, like fiberboard or flakeboard, are extremely porous and really soak up paint. Three and four coats of pigmented paint are sometimes needed to obtain a good solid-looking finish on them. Stains, however, make a fine finish on particleboard without numerous coats. Interior unpainted particleboard can be finished with clear coatings, such as lacquer, polyurethane, shellac, and varnish, for a natural look. Particleboard can be filled with a paste wood filler or spackle to make them smoother.

Before putting an enamel or flat colored-up paint finish on bare particleboard, a wood undercoater should be applied. Otherwise, flaking can occur later. If particleboard is sprayed, a roller set-up should be used to work the wet paint into the surface for best results. *See also* **Paint** and **Plywood.**

Peeling: Paint peels because the surface it was applied to was dirty, oily, or wet, or has become so. Apply paint only to clean, dry surfaces. Look for moisture problems before painting, and correct them before repainting an area that is now peeling. *See* **Prep work.**

Penetrating oil: *See* **Oil finishes.**

Penetration: Generally speaking, oil-based paints, stains, and undercoaters penetrate deeper than water-based products. One reason is that oil-based products take longer to dry, and as liquid, they have more time to penetrate. Don't use fast-drying sealers or undercoaters on surfaces where penetration is important.

There are specially packaged thinning agents, drying oils, that, when added to oil-based paints, help increase their penetration.

Phenolic is a synthetic resin derived from phenol and is used in making coatings. Roller covers with an inner core made of phenolic are usually good-quality, durable covers.

Phosphoric acid is a white or yellowish crystalline solid. It is used as a reducing agent for some paint coatings. It can also be used to etch new aluminum surfaces.

Pigments are the coloring agents in paint. They are very fine powders, either natural or man-made, organic and inorganic.

Pipes: Always remove grease, oil, or water from a pipe before painting it. Do all the necessary chipping and sanding on the pipes. Undercoat any and all bare metal spots with a good metal undercoater. Use a rust-resistant primer on all the prepped rusted areas. An industrial enamel or a rust-fighting enamel are both good finishes for painting exposed pipes.

For painting pipes, don't use too big a paint brush or it will fishtail and not be good for doing fine work. A 3-inch roller set-up and a brush are a fast way to paint small or medium-size exposed pipes. Consider using a segmented or wrap-around roller cover for painting exposed pipes. A painter's mitt is also a good tool for exposed pipes. *See* **Mitt** and **Coal-tar enamels.**

Pitch streaks are resins, usually in softwoods, that bleed to the surface. Remove them with mineral spirits, and when the surface is dry, seal them with shellac or a fast-drying stain-killer. Otherwise, they will bleed through your paint job.

Planking: Whenever there is a lot of ladder work, especially around awkward areas like stairwells, consider using a plank setup. It alleviates having to stand on uncomfortable rungs, dangerous over-reaching, and making frequent trips up and down to relocate the ladder.

A simple plank setup consists of a 6-foot ladder, 4-foot ladder, and a long sturdy board. This eliminates frequent trips up and down a ladder.

There are solid metal or aluminum planks in various lengths, from 8 feet to 20 feet or more. There are also accordion planks (also called pencil planks and scissor planks) that can be pulled apart or together, to lengthen or shorten them. Accordion planks are wobbly when pulled apart and more of a balance and

weight-limit risk than solid metal planks. However, they work well in small areas.

But the most common planking system is simply a strong, sturdy 2x10 or 2x12 board, supported on the rungs of two ladders. For safety and ease, it is recommended that two people set up a planking system. To set up a plank in an interior stairwell, lean an extension ladder against the wall, with a ladder jack if needed, and a 4-foot, 5-foot, or 6-foot ladder on the ground, across from the wall where the extension ladder is. Then, put a plank across the extension ladder rung or ladder jack to the stepladder. Make sure that the plank extends at least 2 feet past the supporting rungs on each side. Now you can reach the ceiling and high walls.

But before using a planking system on high work, do this simple test: Place a 1- or 2-foot-high wooden or concrete block under each end of the plank. Bounce or jump up and down on the plank. If the plank doesn't crack, break, or bend too much, then there is a good chance that it will be safe to use on high work.

Never go over the weight limit for the particular plank you are using! When two or more people are working on a plank, be careful not to have all the weight on one side of the plank.

Plaster is basically a mixture of lime, sand, and water, with fiber sometimes added. The term, plastering, is used loosely in the painting world for any kind of patching that must be mixed on the site and takes two or more passes to complete. This also includes doing stucco patching and bigger exterior and interior patching work. A hawk, trowel, broadknife, and float are tools necessary for doing most plastering work. Stiff brushes are sometimes used to texture plastered areas and feather them into the surroundings to create a match.

Always mix patching plaster according to the manufacturer's specifications. It may be necessary to apply water to an already prepped hole or crack before plastering is started to achieve a better bond.

Always remove old pieces of plaster from lath before plastering over it. Use patching plasters and stucco patching mixes for first or second passes on deep cracks and holes. Undercoating dried new plaster with the right undercoaters is a good idea before applying finish-paint coats. On previously chalky plastered areas or surfaces, consider using a masonry conditioner for the primer coat.

Don't paint wood around wet plaster. If new plaster is not allowed to dry sufficiently, the moisture in the plaster will be drawn into the bare woodwork nearby. The result will be quick blistering of the woodwork's paint.

When plaster is dry, it is not necessarily cured. Newly applied plaster should be given at least thirty days to cure before painting over it, unless the directions on the bag it came from say differently.

Plaster curing is an exothermic reaction, so if it's painted over before it is completely cured, it will create what is known in the trade as a "hot spot," and the paint will deteriorate rapidly here.

Plastering and wallpapering are good second trades for a full-time painter. *See also* **Alkali, Cracks, Floats, Holes, Stucco, Spackle, Quick-setting patching plaster,** and **Vinegar.**

Plaster of paris is a white powder (gypsum) that becomes a paste when water is added to it. It then dries in the air rapidly and becomes hard and brittle. It was originally made in Paris, France, hence its name.

Plaster of paris can be used for patching holes in interiors that are less than one inch in diameter. Don't use plaster of paris where water, moisture, or sunlight can reach it on interior surfaces because it will disintegrate. For these same reasons, don't use plaster of paris on any exterior surfaces or areas. On acoustic ceilings plaster of paris can be used on holes under one inch before acoustic patching texture goes over it. Since plaster of paris sets up quickly, mix only the amount you can use in a few minutes. A small amount of vinegar or milk helps somewhat to slow down the drying time.

Plastic: Generally speaking, most paints don't bond well to plastic surfaces, including plastic laminate. This is especially true on exterior surfaces, where sunlight and water will more rapidly deteriorate paints on plastic surfaces than they would on a different surface. If you feel you must paint on interior plastic surfaces, some epoxy paints may bond well and last longer than other paints.

Plywood: If you want to put a colored finish paint over a bare, unpainted plywood surface or other man-made panel, such as particleboard or fiberboard, ask your paint dealer for a special plywood undercoater that is made specifically for priming plywood. If you can't find one, two or three coats of an exterior wood undercoater can be used as an alternative. Latex flat paints are recommended for use in two or three paint coats as finishes on plywood surfaces over other kinds of pigmented paints. On interior unpainted plywood surfaces, consider using a couple of coats of a clear finish only, or a semi-transparent stain, and a couple of coats of a clear finish over that. *See* **Particleboard.**

Polyurethanes should be used on interior surfaces only, unless they have ultraviolet light protection and are specified for exterior use. They are generally used where a clear coating is preferred on wood surfaces that get heavy use, such as on bar tops, tables, counters, and floors. They are rugged, but they don't age gracefully, and they are not easily removed with strippers. Polyurethane is not recommended for fine furniture or antiques that you feel you someday will refinish, because refinishing could damage the piece.

Apply polyurethanes in a dust-free environment, working as with any varnish, applying quickly and then leveling with long, light brush strokes. Some surfaces may require surface conditioning or sealing before applying polyurethane. Check the label.

Ventilation is important when working with polyurethanes. When spraying them, use a carbon-filter mask. *See also* **Clear Finishes, Floors,** and **Varnishes.**

Pools: For best results and durability, use only those coatings specially formulated for pool areas.

Porcelain fixtures and baked-enamel objects, including sinks, bathtubs, refrigerators, and stoves should not be painted if you are looking for a quality, long-lasting finish. These materials are finished during the manufacturing process, and the result is difficult to duplicate without special materials and equipment. There are special coatings, however, labeled epoxy paints or porcelain paints, if you must try. *See also* **Baked finishes.**

The term "porcelain" is sometimes used by manufacturers to describe the fine, high-gloss surface of their paint. It is not really porcelain, which is a fine, light-colored clay, usually colored and/or glazed before it's fired.

Pot hook or **S-hook** is either a manufactured tool, or one that can be made with a metal coat hanger, used mostly on extension ladders to hold a can of paint so you can work from it. A metal coat-hanger hook will certainly be strong enough to hold a 1-gallon can, but it might not be the best for a 5-gallon can.

Pourstone is a quick-setting patching mix that comes in a powdered form to be mixed with water. It is used mostly for anchoring posts, railings, or bolts into concrete or masonry surfaces.

Prep work is the most important part of painting. Even if the finest undercoaters and finish paints are applied ever so professionally, if the preparatory work has not been done correctly, the finish will not look good. Neither will it last very long.

Prep work is often neglected in the rush to get on with the painting. Indeed, a good prep job can take longer than the painting, but if done right, painting will go smoother and faster. Paint itself will not fill cracks and holes, nor will it adhere to a dirty, oily, mildewed, alligatoring,

Prep first, then paint.

flaking, or peeling surface. If it's not prepped right, you'll be back. So always do the necessary prep work the first time.

For exterior prep work, first remove any hardware, door bells, mail boxes, and the like that easily come off and are not to be painted, or that are in the way. Next, remove screens, shutters, awnings, or other similar things that are in the way of your work. On interiors, instead of removing certain fixtures, such as ceiling and wall lighting fixtures, consider whether it might be easier to lower, move them out, or mask in place and then prep or paint around them.

Wash your surfaces thoroughly. Indoors, use a mild detergent; outdoors, hose things down and scrub them. Where there's heavy dirt, oil, or grease, add T.S.P. (trisodium phosphate) to your cleaning solution. Mineral spirits also remove oil and wax. Remove mildew with a solution of bleach, water, and elbow grease.

After everything is dry, put down drop cloths wherever you will be working. For a lot of scraping on large areas or surfaces, start with a 3- to 40-inch-wide scraper with a knob on it. A stiff putty knife, a 5-in-1 knife, and a chisel blade can also be used to scrape. Wear protective goggles and cloth gloves when scraping. For windows and small trim areas, use a scraper with a double-edge blade. This tool has a wing-nut and usually comes in sizes $1\frac{1}{2}$ inch to $3\frac{1}{2}$ inch. Use a pocket file to sharpen your scraper blades from time to time. For contoured areas, a molding scraper with a teardrop-shaped blade works. Remove old caulking and loose paint in corners with a chisel putty knife, a 5-in-1 knife, or a stiff-bladed putty knife. Open cracks and holes so they can be filled and secured.

To remove old putty from windows, use a flexible putty knife or use a 1-inch-wide double-edge scraper. Remember to scrape or chip parallel to the window sash, and don't push or scrape directly into the window glass, or you may break it! Use power sanders where possible to smooth uneven surfaces, after chipping them. Circular sanders can be used on gutters, downspouts, railings, and large surfaces. Don't leave sanding indentations or swirl marks on wood surfaces. Orbital sanders (called "jitterbugs," in the trade) work well on small areas. Sand all windows and hard-to-reach trim areas with block sanders or by hand with folded sandpaper and elbow grease.

After the sanding is finished, dust off all the areas to be painted. Vacuum where practical.

Before applying glazing compound

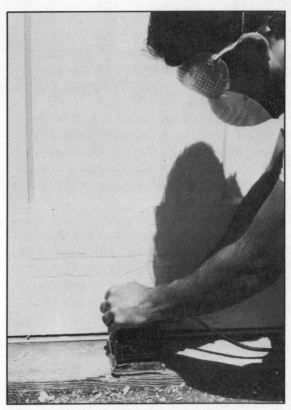

A hand-held sander, or "jitterbug," is great for use on thresholds. Wear goggles and a particle mask to keep dust out of your nose and eyes.

around windows, undercoat them for a better bond. Next, do all the necessary major patching of holes and cracks in the drywall, plaster, or masonry surfaces. Make sure your patches are flush with the surrounding areas and textured the same. Countersink all popped nails and patch them.

Hammer any loose siding back in place. Replace any badly damaged shin-

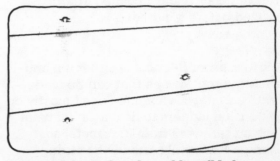

Countersink, sand, and spackle nail holes.

gles. Fill interior wood cracks with wood putty (spackle works well on interior wood where the finish is a flat or enamel paint), and fill exterior ones with an appropriate spackle. When the spackle has completely dried, sand it smooth and flush with the surrounding surface. Load up your caulking gun and caulk all the necessary seams, cracks, and other areas

Chalking on masonry surface

that aren't patched or spackled over and are under ¼ inch deep or wide. (Surfaces to be coated with a clear finish generally do not require patching.)

Scrape, chip, and sand all rusted areas that haven't been prepped yet. Then use a rust-resistant primer or red-lead primer on all the rusted areas after dusting them. Use a masonry conditioner on any masonry surfaces or plastered areas where a better finish-paint bond is desired after sanding and dusting them, especially if they were chalky with alkali deposits.

Next, and finally, walk around the job site and double-check all the prep work. Attend to anything missed. Don't start painting prematurely. *See also* **Blisters, Burning, Caulking, Drywall, Putty, Sandpaper, Holes, Cracks, Water-blasting, Mildew, Rust, Plastering, Wood, Metals, Masonry, Drops, Undercoaters, Quick-setting patching plaster, Spackling, Exteriors,** and **Interiors.**

Primers: *See* **Undercoaters.**

Pumice is a fine abrasive powder used for rubbing down finishes to create a satin sheen. Also, the better hand cleaners contain pumice.

Putty, also called glazing compound, is made of linseed oil and whiting. Basically, it's a doughlike cement.

In preparing a window for reglazing, chip and scrape the old glazing compound off, working parallel with the sash at all times. Don't apply pressure directly into the window pane! After you have chipped off all the loose or old putty, sand the sash and dust the window well. Undercoat all the places where the putty will go. Undercoating produces a better, longer-lasting bond, because it seals the wood and keeps it from drying out the putty.

When the undercoater is dry, it's time for puttying or glazing. Take out of the can only the amount of putty to be used in fifteen minutes. Then put the lid back. Get yourself a glazing knife (a special tool with a bent blade) or a 1½-inch to 2½-inch flexible putty knife. Roll the putty into a ball of uniform consistency. Take part of the rolled-up ball and press or pinch it with your fingers and thumb into the sash areas of the window, moving it along and creating an even putty-line. Next, use your glazing tool and press down very firmly, creating a putty-line angle of 45 degrees or so. Move parallel along the window sash, pressing your putty in. Run your glazing tool again along your putty line and smooth it out, without creating voids in your putty line. Use either your knife or your fingers to remove any excess putty from the window glass, being careful not to mar your putty line. Discard any putty that doesn't go along the putty line, or add it to your putty ball and work it back in. Longer glazing lines can go faster if you form the putty into a string roll before applying it. Sometimes small amounts of water added to putty can aid in smoothing it out. Don't add too much, or it just gets sloppy. When putty sticks to a putty knife, try moistening it. If the whole can of putty is too dry, you may want to add some linseed oil to it. When putty is too wet and oily, you may want to add some powdered whiting (calcium carbonate or chalk) to it.

For best results, wait seven to twenty-one days, depending on weather conditions, before painting over a freshly glazed window. When paint is applied to putty that is not completely dry, wrinkling or curdling of the paint film may occur. Lightly sand dried putty before painting over it.

On exteriors, use glazing compound labeled for exterior use, and always shape glazing on a window at an angle, so that water will run off it. Don't leave the lid off a putty can, unless you are drying out a mixture that's too wet. Incidentally, leaving lids off putty, glazing compounds, and spackle is one of the most common mistakes people make.

Putty is also used to fill countersunk nail holes and cracks. It is a good idea to undercoat these areas before applying putty. Give glazing compounds used on deep nail holes or deep cracks, fifty to sixty hours to dry before painting over them, unless the label on a particular putty can says differently.

There are premixed colored or already tinted putties that can be bought for use on woods that have been finished with clear or colored semi-transparent stains. Some are labeled with a name for use on a particular kind of wood or with a certain color. It is sometimes a good idea to apply putty on a wood surface before the finish coat of a semi-transparent stain or clear coating has been applied to prevent "flashing" (differences in sheen or texture) from occurring. However, some people do just the opposite and like the results.

Generally speaking, dark gray or bluish putties are used on aluminum or steel windows, whereas white or off-white putties are used on wooden windows. *See* **Spackle** and **Water putty.**

Quick-setting patching plaster

comes in powdered form to be mixed up with water on the spot. Mix up only the amount you can use in five to seven minutes. Most quick-setting plasters start drying fast in five to twenty minutes and usually turn a darker brown or grayish color when completely dried. A white liquid grout additive will slow down the drying time; so will milk, somewhat.

Quick-setting plaster can be used on interior surfaces; however, for an exterior surface, check that the product label says it is recommended for outside usage. Don't use quick-setting plasters in the place of stucco cement, or the plaster originally used on a particular wall or surface, when you're covering large areas. Quick-fixer patching mixes can be used quite well in deep holes and cracks on wood surfaces

Before each new batch of quick plaster is mixed up, make sure your buckets and mixing tools are clean. Failure to do so will cause the patching mix to dry faster, and the tools and buckets will be harder to clean later.

Work as quickly as possible when applying quick patches and remember that they are usually hard to sand over when they're completely dry. It is a good idea to sand quick patches right before they completely harden. *See* **Holes, Cracks, Plastering, Hawk,** and **Trowel.**

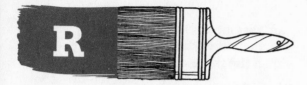

Rags: Always have a rag on hand whenever you are doing any preparatory or painting work. Rags can be bought rather inexpensively at paint stores in 3-, 5-, and 10-pound packages. However, old sheets and towels make good rags when they are cut up. Have some tough, textured rags, as well as some smoother ones. Put aside certain rags to be used for semi-transparent staining only. Use dirty rags for wiping up bad spills or drips and clean rags for small drips and spills. Use your cleanest rags for fine enamel or clear coating work.

Oily or thinner-soaked rags should not be left around open flames, or indoors after quitting time. Oily rags can spontaneously combust, so either dry them out before discarding or keep them submerged in water.

Razor blades: If you're a professional painter, you'll use a lot of razor blades for scraping, scoring, and cutting, so buy them in bulk and discard them when they dull. Don't store razor blades any old way, as you or somebody else could get cut when reaching for something else. Instead, put them in their wrappers and store them in a secure box or a can with a lid on it. Before discarding an old blade, wrap the edge in masking tape. It is a good idea to wear cloth gloves for protection when working with razor blades. When scraping windows with razor blades, discard dull and rusted razor blades as they may leave scrape marks on the glass.

Keep in mind that a little water put on water-based paint drips or overspray on windows will make them come off more easily, even if they are already completely dried out. Mineral spirits or denatured alcohol can work the same way on oil-based paint drips or overspray. Apply before scraping.

There is a razor-blade scraper tool that holds a razor blade for scraping. It's inexpensive and makes scraping with razor blades much easier. A razor-blade wallpaper scraper can also be used with good results to scrape paint from windows.

Red-labeled paints: Be cautious with red-labeled paints because they are flammable and explosive, usually with flash points below 80 degrees! Read all the information and cautions on red-label paints before using them.

Red-lead primers are very dense and heavy compared with other paints and primers. They are made from lead and are deep red in color. Red-lead primers are used mostly for their rust-resisting qualities. They were used frequently many years ago for priming gutters and on all rusted areas; they're now illegal in many places because they contain lead. Remember to paint over a surface that has been primed with a red-lead undercoater within forty-five hours for best results.

Red-lead primers are excellent primers for fighting rust and should be considered, especially for very bad cases of rust.

Reducers: Certain brick and metal undercoaters require special thinning agents, or reducers, to thin them and to clean up tools used with them. Reducers are somewhat expensive, but they are necessary for certain primers and paints.

Redwood: Bare unpainted redwood commonly has stains caused by moisture. Use a 50 percent to 65 percent solution of denatured alcohol and water in one or two passes to get rid of these stains before painting over them. Redwood has a reputation for bleeding through flats and enamels, so use one or two coats of a wood undercoater or a fast-drying stain killer before applying a pigmented paint.

Redwood is commonly stained with a semi-transparent or solid-body stain in a familiar reddish brown. Alternatively, a weathered, gray look on an exterior bare redwood surface can be brought on quickly by using a bleaching oil, a commercial bleach with a gray color in it. Many paint stores carry special undercoaters, primers, sealers, and finish paints designed especially for redwood surfaces such as redwood shingles, siding, and decks.

Refinishing: The first step in refinishing furniture is to determine whether it's needed at all. Many old pieces of furniture just need cleaning up, which can be done with a mild detergent or mineral spirits. Test your cleaner on an inconspicuous area first to make sure it does not harm the finish. Valuable antiques should be looked over by an expert before refinishing; otherwise you may be reducing the value of your furniture.

If you do decide to refinish, begin by removing any hardware, mirrors, and so forth. To help determine the previous clear finish coating used on a surface or area, consider making the following test: Take a cotton swab with some denatured alcohol on it. Apply the denatured alcohol to an unwaxed part of the surface in question and let it stay for a minute or longer. If the finish rubs off or softens up, then it's most likely shellac. To test for a clear lacquer finish, do the same test using lacquer thinner. If the lacquer thinner doesn't do anything to the finish, then it is most likely a plastic, urethane, or varnish of some sort. Any of these finishes can be removed, with varying degrees of ease, with a paint stripper. At least now you know what you're removing.

For directions on stripping, *see* **Paint remover.** Once the old finish is off, and

any residue of the paint remover is washed off with mineral spirits, you can finish the piece as if it were new. You probably don't have to sand it, however; if it was sanded originally, the paint remover has not changed that.

It's not unusual for furniture to require some structural or cosmetic repair. Now's the time to do that. A specialty tool called a burn-in knife used with lacquer sticks can often fix dents, burn marks, scratches, and gouges on wood surfaces. Keep in mind, though, that old furniture has character. Minor surface blemishes can be regarded as part of the patina.

You might consider staining the wood if you want to change its color, or just even out variations. The most commonly available stains are oil-based pigmented stains, which you usually apply with a clean cloth and wipe off. These stains color by depositing pigment in the pores and crevices of the wood, so the more you apply the muddier the surface may appear. There's some sense, if you don't know exactly what you want, in starting light and progressing darker. But if you know you want a dark color, buy a dark-colored stain. *See* **Stains.**

Once the color is as you want it, you can apply your clear finish. The choices include oil, shellac, lacquer, and varnish, which can be based on natural or synthetic resins. For choosing and applying these, *see* **Clear coatings** and **Oil finishes.**

Consider using the wire method that is found in the brushing section of this book when applying a clear coating to your refinishing project. Also consider using a seal-coat in your refinishing operation. *See* **Floors.**

For best results let a clear finish cure for fifteen days or longer before rubbing it out with mineral oil and a mild abrasive. Rottenstone can achieve a high gloss; pumice gives you a satin gloss. Use light, even strokes along the grain. Don't lap over your previously rubbed areas, and always rub from a polished area into an unpolished area. Don't rub too vigorously or apply too much elbow grease, or you could rub all the way through the finish. If possible use a polishing-type pad or a lint-free, soft-cotton type of cloth or rag.

Resins are hard, translucent substances that dissolve in organic solvents, like turpentine and mineral spirits, but not in water. In paint and varnish formulas, resins add hardness and durability to the film. Organic resins are secretions from trees, either recent or not. Some natural resins are fossil remains from primeval trees, including extinct species. Synthetic resins can be produced to combine ideal characteristics, and thus have revolutionized the paint industry.

Copal, amber, rosin, and damar are some natural resins. Many varnish and lacquer formulas include one or more of these. Synthetic resins are acrylic, alkyd, epoxy, phenolic, polyurethane, and vinyl, to mention a few. The label will say what resins were used in the making of a particular paint. Many times the name of the paint will identify the principal resin used. Acrylic, latex, or vinyl paints are water-based. Alkyd is the predominant resin in today's oil-based paints. Polyurethane is used in strong man-made clear finishes.

Rollers have not eliminated the use of brushes in painting, but they certainly do a faster, better job on large areas. A professional roller set-up consists of a handle (sometimes referred to as a "cage"), a cover (which slips over the cage), and a 9-inch screen that fits in a 5-gallon can (or a 7-inch screen that fits in a 2-gallon can) to roll the paint onto the roller. Roller trays are good for small areas, but they're awkward to move around, filling them up repeatedly takes time, and they don't provide an even load to the roller the way a screen does. If you use a tray, consider adding a screen to it.

Roller covers come in natural and syn-

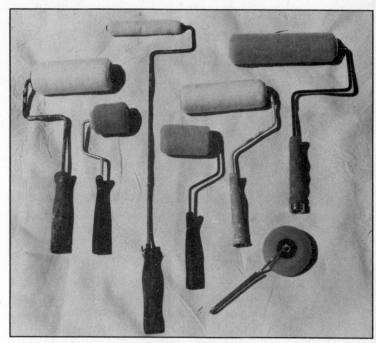

Rollers come in all sizes and shapes. The circular roller on the right front is called a `corner roller' (for cutting in corners where two walls meet). The skinny roller in the middle is called a "toilet," or "hot dog," roller.

thetic naps. Natural covers are sheepskin, lambswool, and mohair. They usually cost more than similar synthetic roller covers. Use natural roller covers or blended good-quality polyester naps with oil-based paints. Don't use a lambswool cover with water-based paints, or it could get matted. Use synthetic roller covers with water-based paints. Don't use synthetic naps with lacquers or other hot solvents, such as acetone, benzene, and naphtha, as they could get eaten up. However, synthetic roller covers can be used with oil-based paints that have been thinned with mineral spirits or turpentine without incurring any damage.

Remember that quality roller covers work better, faster, and give more consistent paint coverage than bargain-basement ones. A cheap roller cover will splatter considerably more than a quality one and pieces of fuzz will fall out of it and get into your paint.

Rollers come in sizes of ¹/₂ inch to 4¹/₂

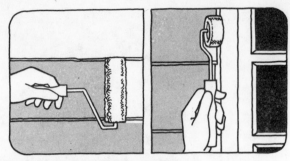

Use the right roller for the job.

inches in diameter and 3 inches, 7 inches, 9 inches, and even 18 inches in length. There is a corner roller, sometimes called a "donut roller," for cutting in corner areas and siding strips. There are small "toilet rollers," which are designed for getting behind cramped places. And there are wraparound and segmented roller covers designed exclusively for rolling out columns, pipes, and other round things

Roller covers come in a variety of thicknesses and textures. Rollers generally leave a stippled texture. The thicker the nap, the more paint it will carry and the more texture it will leave, hiding minute surface imperfections on a smooth wall.

Use a thin roller cover (under $1/4$ inch nap) for gloss and semi-gloss finishes on smooth surfaces, such as plaster, floors, and some walls. Use covers $3/8$ inch to $3/4$ inch thick for flat paints on medium-smooth surfaces, including most interior walls, interior light stucco, and sandy textured surfaces. For rough or porous surfaces like bricks, rough plaster, stucco, cinder block, and fences, use roller covers 1-inch to $1^1/2$-inch thick. There are special roller covers designed for rolling acoustic ceilings; however, spraying is recommended for painting acoustic ceilings instead of rolling them out.

Some paint stores sell small, padlike two-sided, foam rollers that can be used for painting wrought-iron fences and handrails.

On new roller covers that have fuzz and hairs that can come off and get in your fine work, especially enamels and clear finishes, consider doing the following: Wrap the roller cover in masking tape completely and then take it off, along with the loose fuzz and hairs. If a slip-on roller cover doesn't fit snugly on a particular cage, consider pulling the cage's spokes a little farther out to remedy the situation.

If possible, clean your roller covers at the end of the painting workday. However, if you don't clean them, at least soak them in the appropriate solvent. Completely submerge each roller, without sunlight or air reaching it. Don't soak a roller like this for more than a day. Use a roller spinner tool for cleaning roller covers faster and better. A wire brush or a roller comb is good for cleaning and combing a roller cover.

After cleaning a roller cover, make sure it is stored standing up on its end for quicker drying and also so that the cover doesn't get matted. After thorough drying, a roller cover can be stored for greater protection in a plastic bag or aluminum foil.

Consider throwing away any roller handle or cage that leaks paint or no longer rolls smoothly on the walls or ceilings. Roller cages that squeak can sometimes be cured by lubricating them with petroleum jelly, hand cream, or grease.

Get a more expensive roller handle or cage over a bargain basement variety, as rolling and durability of the better-quality handles and cages are well worth it. Compression-type roller handles are recommended over the cheaper wing-nut variety types.

Make sure the roller handle you choose can screw into an extension pole. Extension poles usually make rolling go faster and put less strain on the body overall. The recommendation is for the adjustable aluminum or fiberglass kind. If you paint full-time, you'll need a couple of different lengths; if you're painting around your own home, choose a pole that adjusts from 3 feet to 6 feet or so.

Rolling: Like anything else in painting, rolling takes practice. When painting a ceiling or a wall, plan on finishing diagonally or crosswise to where you started. Dip the roller into the paint about halfway up the roller cover. Now, push and pull the roller up and down the screen, each time dipping it into the paint, until it is uniformly covered. Two or three dips are usually enough. Next, pull the roller out of the bucket, turning it slowly in the air to avoid drips falling off as it is carried. Put the roller against the ceiling or wall and roll out a letter M, W, or N in a 2- or 3-square-foot area. Dip the roller again and make a smaller letter M,

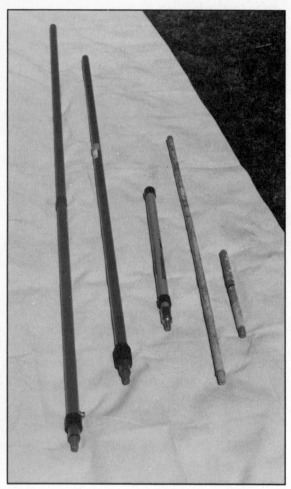

Rolling poles come in different sizes for different jobs.

When rolling, use the appropriate rolling setup for the job at hand. L to R: 1-gallon bucket with a 3-inch roller and grate, 2-gallon bucket with a 7-inch roller and grate, and a 5-gallon bucket with a 9-inch roller and grate. Front: A rolling tray and an inexpensive plastic throw-away rolling tray that fits snugly into it.

For large areas where spraying is not an option, consider using a power-feed roller. This rig utilizes a compressor, which pumps paint from your can up a hose to a special roller. The paint fills the inside of the roller and exudes through the nap of the roller cover. It provides very even coverage and of course it's fast, because you never have to go back to load up. Even though these rollers have been around for a while now, few full-time painters use them. They are a little awkward, with the tube attached to the roller handle, and heavy. However, for large jobs, they are an option, and if they are improved and made less expensive, more people will discover their benefits. *See also* **Clean-up** and **Rolling.**

W, or N next to the other pattern. Next roll out the two patterns uniformly up and down. Then simply proceed likewise across the entire ceiling or wall. Dry-roll your last rolled areas, evening them out and correcting holidays, or missed areas.

Start rolling in an upward motion on a

wall. Always apply paint from a dry area to a wet area. Maintain a wet edge, overlapping your work by 40 percent, as you progress. Use light strokes for fine work. Thick roller stipple or edge lines may be hard to feather out completely. Don't over-roll: Aim for an even thickness by rolling in increasingly large areas with less and less paint on the roller, but stop before the roller is too dry and dip it again. Don't spin a roller at the end of a roll, as overspray will end up everywhere you don't want it.

When putting your first rolling areas on a wall or ceiling, don't put them too close to cut-in lines near trimwork and corner or ceiling areas, especially when working with enamel paints. Cut in before you start rolling, especially when using enamel paints. Dead flat finishes can be an exception.

Rolling out of a paint tray is okay in small kitchens and bathrooms or in small or cramped areas. However, the recommendation is to use a 5-gallon can, or at least a deuce (2-gallon bucket), fitted with a screen. Rolling out of a 5-gallon container without a screen should be done only where paint flying everywhere, overspray, drips, and spills do not matter, as on some new construction jobs.

When doing any spraying of large areas or surfaces, a roller set-up is a good backup and touch-up device to have around.

Roller stipple marks and lap marks don't look good on clear finishes, so it is best not to use a roller with them. However, floors are an exception.

Don't stop rolling in the middle of a wall or surface. Instead, complete a side, or finish to a corner, or some other good squaring-off place. Don't leave a roller set-up in the middle of a room or near a door if people are walking around. Instead, keep your material against or near a wall.

Don't leave a roller out of the paint material or bucket unattended or uncovered for more than a minute outdoors or five minutes indoors. Never leave a roller set-up exposed directly to the sun. If you must leave a roller set-up in the sun, then cover and protect it. *See also* **Rollers** and **Clean-up.**

Roofs: Generally speaking, a painted roof needs repainting every five years. Protecting a roof by painting, sealing or otherwise treating it is a good investment in preventive maintenance. Cedar shakes or shingles should be coated when they start to become grayish and lose their natural orange-brown color. However in hot climates, cedar shakes should be treated when they become bleached-out. Replace damaged cedar or other kinds of wooden shakes or shingles before coating or treating a cedar or wooden roof. Stains, wood preservatives, water-repellent sealers, and other appropriate paint coatings all can be used on bare wooden roofs.

Special roof coatings are formulated for just about any surface or building material found on the roof of a house or building. Most mobile home roofs are made of aluminum. Aluminum paint coatings reflect heat and thus help to insulate a building against heat.

For best results paint a slanted roof from top to bottom. There is available a device called a ladder hook that, when connected to an extension ladder, enables the ladder to fit securely onto a roof peak. This way, you can work on a slanted roof with something positive to grip and stand on. One piece of an extension ladder can also be secured on a roof by tying it down on one or both ends to trees or a strong, stable object.

Spraying should be considered as the painting or application method used for treating roofs whenever practical and possible.

On hot days working on the roof in the early morning hours is a definite recommendation. *See also* **Woods, Metals, Aluminum,** and **Exteriors.**

Rottenstone is basically a brownish colored, extra-fine, abrasive powder for hand-polishing glossy surfaces. It is similar to pumice, but finer. Rottenstone is used on refinishing work and over clear finishes. A high gloss can be achieved on a completely dried clear finish by using rottenstone with a rubbing oil on it. Wait eight days or longer before using rottenstone on a surface that has previously been rubbed with pumice and a rubbing oil. *See also* **Refinishing.**

Rough-rider is a slang term for a specially designed staining brush. In addition to capacious bristles on its main surface, it has a separate row of bristles for cutting in edges or strips, such as wood siding. The brush is dipped into stain, and puts out a goodly amount of stain when applied to a surface. A person can work stain into a surface thoroughly, with plenty of elbow grease, when using a rough-rider. When you have a lot of staining to do, you might want to use this brush.

Rust results from the oxidation of ferrous metals. It takes place, to some extent, whenever a ferrous metal is exposed to air, but it is accelerated by moisture. Paint can inhibit the formation of rust by sealing a metal surface from air and moisture.

Where rust already exists, a surface must be prepped before painting. First scrape down any loose rust. This can be done by wire-brushing, hand-sanding, disc-grinding, sandblasting, using cold chisels and, in mild cases, liquid rust removers. A blow torch can help crystallize rust for scraping.

After treating rusted areas, wash them and let them dry well. When dry, immediately apply a rust-resistant primer or undercoater. Most quality rust-resistant primers are slower drying, red in color, and penetrate well. For severe cases of rust, apply two or more coats.

A rust-fighting exterior enamel that says so on its label or an exterior industrial enamel are both good finish paints for use over treated and primed rusted areas. Use two or three finish coats for best results and greater durability. *See* **Metals** and **Paint.**

Sal-soda (a hydrated sodium carbonate) is sometimes used to remove soot, dirt, and grease from a surface.

Sand is called "rock" in the trade when it is used in plaster and stucco mixtures, or when it is added to paint to create textured surfaces. Sand can be bought in bags or bulk and is graded according to the size of the grains. When matching textured or masonry surfaces with patching materials, compare grain sizes. If you add sand to a paint, don't add more than 45 percent by volume.

Sandblasting is a powerful means of cleaning surfaces, such as brick, masonry, wood, and metal. The end result is bare material. Sandblasting is costly, messy, noisy, and potentially damaging to the surroundings, so before deciding on it, make sure you've considered less radical procedures.

Sanding and sandpaper: On interiors, the usual sanding to be done is the doors, casings, non-textured ceilings, non-textured walls, cabinets, mouldings, baseboards, window trim, and any trimwork that doesn't have a textured surface.

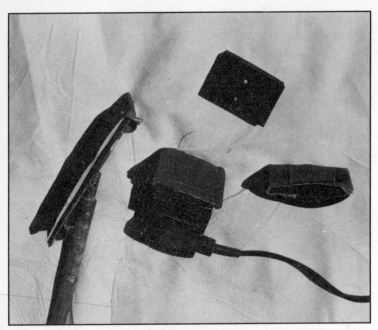

For sanding, use the following appropriate tools. Rear: foam sanding block. Front L to R: sanding pole, power hand-held sander, and hard rubber sanding block.

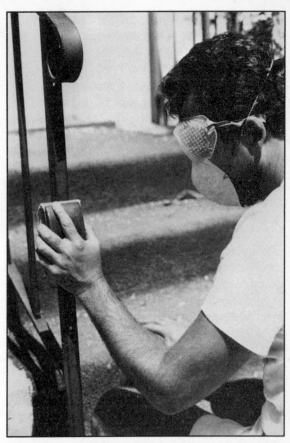

When using a block sander on a railing, wear both goggles to protect your eyes and a particle mask to protect your nose from minute metal filings.

There's also the sanding of furniture to be finished or refinished

On exteriors, the usual sanding is the trimwork, fascia board, windows, doors, casings, gutters and downspouts. Most wood siding requires little or no sanding.

Before sanding, make sure the area around where you're working is prepared for the mess that sanding inevitably makes: Dust seems to end up everywhere. Cover what needs to be, including your nose and mouth with a particle mask. *See* **Masks.**

Remove any loose paint, dirt, grease, and oil from a surface before sanding it. Don't try to accomplish with sandpaper what you should with a scraper. And don't try sanding a damp surface, unless you're wet-sanding, which is a good technique for rubbing out a clear coating.

Sandpaper is classified by grit: the higher the number, the finer the grit. For most prep work, 60-grit or 80-grit is coarse and 120-grit is a fine as you need to go. For finish work 220-grit and finer can be used. The abrasive material itself can be garnet, which is best for hand-sanding wood; aluminum oxide, which is suited for power-sanding; and silicon carbide, for the finer grits, often on paper that can hold up to wet-sanding.

The grit is applied to the paper in one of two densities: open-coat and closed-coat, the latter containing more abrasive particles per square inch. Closed-coat density cuts faster, but it tends to clog in sappy woods, like pine, or under power. Open-coat density, also called "production paper," is designed for power sanding.

If you use a lot of a particular grit sandpaper, you may find it economical to buy a sleeve of it containing 100 sheets. Sometimes masking tape applied to the back of sandpaper will make it last longer. Sandpaper can be stored quite well in an old record album cover, otherwise known as a "painter's sandwich." Or it can be stored in its original sleeve. Store sandpaper flat. Don't store it exposed to direct sunlight or moisture.

To cut sandpaper, fold it in half, crease it, and tear it along a sharp corner. Don't fold the grit sides together and then sand with it. Fold sandpaper in thirds for hand sanding; this way it won't slip around. For greater flexibility pull the sandpaper sheets once or twice over a long sharp corner, with the grit side up. Use a wire brush to clean sandpaper when it gets clogged. This way you can get more mileage from your sandpaper.

When hand-sanding, consider wearing cloth gloves and using a sanding block, which ideally is a piece of cork, rubber, or felt, comfortable in the hand and shaped to match the surface you're sanding.

A sanding pole can be effective on large or hard-to-reach areas. This tool has a wooden handle that is 3 feet or 4 feet long, with a swivel-mounted pad for hold-

Sandpaper comes in different grit, or rock, textures. L to R: 220 grit (very smooth), 80 grit (medium), and 36 grit (very rough). **The black paper in the back is called emery cloth.**

ing sandpaper. It takes a little skill and coordination to change the sandpaper on one of these. If you are doing a lot of pole work, get your whole body into it, not just your arms and shoulders.

When doing very fine work or refinishing, wrap a clean rag around your hand and lightly feel the surface for any missed sanded areas that may need further attention. When sanding wooden furniture, antiques, tables, and the like, don't bear down too hard on any square edges or corners, or you may round them over. Always sand *with* the grain when sanding wood.

Most sanding in the painter's world can and should be done by machine. There are three basic types of portable power sanders: belt sanders, disc sanders, and orbital sanders. Use belt and disc sanders only for rough work and gross material removal. Disc sanders especially leave unsightly sanding marks. Orbital sanders get the most use in prep work for painting. Sometimes called "jitterbugs," they orbit back and forth at high speed, and if used properly will leave no indentations or swirl marks.

Liquid sandpapers can be used quite well on repaints after some sanding is done. Although liquid sandpapers create a good paint bond when they are used liberally on a painted gloss surface, they do not smooth a surface the way real sandpaper does. Be sure there is plenty of ventilation when using liquid sandpaper.

It is a good idea to sand lightly before and in-between coats of enamels and clear coatings. Sanding an undercoater helps to achieve a smooth, even gloss on a surface that is to be enameled. If you are sanding over painted areas and your sandpaper should start removing the paint, consider the following possibilities: The paint is not fully dried yet; your sandpaper is too coarse; the paint never stuck well to begin with and it all needs to be removed for best results.

If sanding seems to take too long to achieve the bare surface or smoothness that you want, you may want to consider first sandblasting, waterblasting, using paint removers, or doing blow-torching as other preparatory methods.

Sanding sealer is a clear material applied to wood to seal the pores. It is easy to sand, powders up readily, and provides a good, smooth ground for applying certain clear coatings that do not themselves sand well. There are special sanding sealers for lacquer and sanding sealers for alkyd varnish, for instance, when one of these is to be the top coat.

Spraying is a fast and efficient way to apply sanding sealers. Most sanding sealers can be thinned down a bit for spraying. *See also* **Woods, Lacquer,** and **Refinishing.**

Sash refers to the trim that immediately surrounds window panes. A sash brush is a narrow, angled brush ideally suited for cutting in sash.

Satin refers to the degree of sheen between flat and semi-gloss finishes. In residential work satin is one of the most popular choices for interior trimwork. But for greater protection, whether inside or out, use a semi-gloss or gloss enamel instead.

Sawdust is good to use for cleaning up paint remover, especially on intricate surfaces that are hard to wipe clean. Sprinkle on the sawdust, let it absorb the paint remover, and brush it off. Do the same for paint residue in buckets. Sawdust can also be used (packed in sandbags) for walking on when placed over a shingled or tiled roof to prevent the materials from breaking.

Scaffolding: On most homes scaffolding is not necessary. Extension ladders,

ladder jacks and planks can usually handle residential height requirements (*see* **Planking**). Wheeled scaffolding can be very effective in large commercial applications. But before renting scaffolding, consider whether you really need it. Scaffolding is costly and time-consuming to set up right.

Inspect all parts of scaffolding before you use any of them. Don't use any cracked, broken, or split pieces.

Anchor scaffolding approximately every 28 feet of length, and every 18 feet of height to the wall. Brace it every 30 feet of height. Have guard railings on the scaffolding at the top and at the ends. Try to have at least a 2-foot overlap on planks used on scaffolding set-ups whenever possible and practical.

Don't force scaffolding braces or parts to fit in place, and never overload a scaffolding set-up beyond the recommended weight limits. Don't change or modify scaffolding by removing braces, uprights, and so forth.

Scrapers: Sometimes it seems that more of a professional painter's time is spent with a scraper and sandpaper than with a roller and brush. Indeed, prep work is the unavoidable first step to a quality job, and most prep work, at least on repaint

Flaking or cracking is similar to peeling in looks, but it is not as advanced a deterioration. It occurs from extreme water damage, or "alligatoring," left untreated.

In the preparation of a painted wooden surface, you may find a cracked or chipped look that resembles the hide of an alligator. "Alligatoring" can be caused by too much moisture on a surface or by putting an enamel paint over a flat paint or a flat paint over a high-sheen paint.

jobs, involves scraping. A scraper can be a wing-nut variety or it can simply be a putty knife or 5-in-1 knife, and on sash and other molded trim you may even find a use for a homemade scraper, ground to fit the contour of your work surface. Larger, flat areas are best scraped with a long-handled scraper that has a knob over the scraper blade for applying pressure with your other hand. Always pull these scrapers, rather than push them. It's a good idea to carry a file in your tool kit to sharpen a scraper blade. This will save time, effort, and money on replacement blades. *See also* **Prep work.**

Screens should be cleaned well with a wire brush before painting. A zinc-dust or other metal primer should be applied next. Besides paint, consider a clear coating as a finish treatment for screens. If you brush out a wire screen, do so with a somewhat dry brush, painting in every direction alternately. Avoid putting too much paint on and clogging up screen-wire hole areas. It might be easier taking window or door screens down, coding them, putting them up against a wall and spraying them.

If you drip paint onto a screen while painting a nearby area, try removing it with a coarse rag dampened with mineral spirits or lacquer thinner if it is an oil-based paint and still wet. Be careful not to damage or break the screen mesh. Use water for a water-based wet paint. If these methods don't work, or if the paint has hardened, use paint remover on it. Dirt or mud has been used to remove wet paint drips on wire screens, concrete, bricks, and asphalt surfaces, and works quite well in many cases. A wire brush may be of help also with the above methods.

Scuff marks can be hard to remove. Apply a stain killer or a shellac primer in two or three passes over them, and they shouldn't bleed through the finish paint.

Sealers: *See* **Undercoaters.**

Semi-gloss is the paint sheen between high-gloss and flat. When you want more protection for a surface but don't want a high shine, consider using a semi-gloss paint. On exteriors, semi-gloss weathers to a satin look in time.

Shelf-life is the length of time a product can sit around and still be good for use. Age compromises a paint's adhesiveness. Don't use a can of paint that has a thick skin, lumps, a foul odor, or color separation.

Shellac is gathered from insect deposits on trees indigenous to India. There are basically two kinds available to painters and finishers: clear-coated shellac and bleached, white shellac (primer-sealer). Shellac is soluble in alcohol, but not in water, mineral spirits, or turpentine. You can buy clear-coated shellac in granular or flake form and dissolve it in alcohol, which makes a fresher mix, or purchase already prepared cans from paint and hardware stores. These cans are usually dated; don't use old shellac.

Shellac has excellent adhesive qualities, is fast-drying, and forms a good-quality film. White shellac is often employed as a stain-killer on interior surfaces to seal problem areas like scuff marks, water damage, and sap pockets. Clear-coated shellac is a good-loooking finish itself, imparting a warm, venerable look and feel to furniture.

Apply clear-coated shellac with a quick brush. It's very volatile compared to paints and varnishes, so an area can be dry before you're finished brushing it. Just apply thin coats and keep moving. Because shellac is so quick-drying, dust is usually not a problem with it, unlike other clear coatings.

Shellac is not a good exterior finish, nor is it recommended where any kind of alcohol may contact it, because it will dissolve. Don't use a water-based paint over a shellac primer-sealer unless a particular label says differently.

Shelves: If they can be removed, it is a good idea to remove shelves and label them in order on a not-to-be painted area. Then prep and paint them leaning them up against a wall to dry. If they can't be removed, you may have difficulty fitting your brush into the tight spaces of a shelving area. Consider cutting off the handle of a brush, so it will fit.

Shield: A paint-shield blade is typically 18 inches to 36 inches long and is usually made of plastic or aluminum. It is used for some cut-in work and for painting near baseboards, carpets, corners, and other similar trimwork areas. Remember to clean or wipe the paint off a paint-shield blade whenever you pick it up. Otherwise, the wet paint on the blade will get on the surface you are trying to keep it from.

Shingles: Bare, unpainted shingles can soak up stains quite rapidly, often covering only 90 square feet to 110 square feet per gallon. Cedar is probably the thirstiest shingle wood.

Shingles can be dipped in a solution of stain before they are nailed. When they are already in place, spraying with an airless sprayer is recommended, because the sprayed paint can get in all the nooks and crannies and other hard-to-get-at places. However, if you do brush and roll shingles before they're applied, don't forget to paint the underside. Paint shingles in place from top to bottom, being careful to catch the edges.

Don't use semi-transparent or solid-body stains over flat- or enamel-painted shingles, as the stain won't penetrate or bond well. Before applying an enamel or flat finish to bare or painted shingles, apply an exterior oil-based wood undercoater first, then apply one or two finish coats of flat or enamel paint for best results.

Wire brushes, scrapers, and water blasting from a downward angle (don't lift the shingles!) are all good preparatory methods for preparing shingles for painting.

Wood preservatives and water-repellent silicone sealers are other coatings that can be used for finishes on bare wood shingles where a natural look and some protection are wanted. *See also* **Roofs.**

Shutters should be taken down and washed with a hose and brush before painting. They are painted quite easily with a spray set-up, in combination with a brush. They can also be brushed out right in place, but that usually takes more time.

Shutters are very noticeable and can attractively accent a house when painted a contrasting or complementary color. They are usually done in a semi-gloss or high-gloss enamel to dress up the flat paint of the house.

Undercoat all bare wood areas with an exterior oil-based wood undercoater before applying colored-up finish paint coats on shutters. *See also* **Louvers.**

Silicone has high lubricity and extreme weather repellency. It is used in some modern caulking compounds.

Soybean oil is a semi-drying oil used in paints as a stabilizer and balancer. *See also* **Drying oils.**

Spackle is a ready-to-use patching compound. Exterior spackle can be used on exteriors and interiors, but don't use interior spackle outside or on any exterior surfaces. Don't use spackle on very rough surfaces, such as stucco or textured surfaces. Spackle works best on smooth walls, ceilings, trimwork, and wood. Spackle can be used with good results on interior areas that have been plastered, and on smooth masonry surfaces.

Spackle can sometimes be used as an alternative to using putty for filling nail holes after an undercoater has been applied. If you choose this method, make sure you apply the spackle in two or three passes, and make sure you sand the dried spackle flush to the surface. Spackle can be used to smooth over some walls or ceilings that have had wallpaper

Before spackling a fascia board

Same fascia board after spackling

removed from them. Spackle that has dried in a crack or hole must be undercoated before an enamel finish goes over it, otherwise flashing can occur.

For best results: Don't take out of the spackle can any more spackle than you can use in eight to ten minutes time. Don't leave the lid off a spackle can for more than a minute, and even less in direct sunlight. Don't put unused spackle back in the can if it has been out for more than five minutes. Throw it away.

When you're working with spackle, be sure to lay drop cloths to catch the excess. A flexible putty knife and a flexible broad knife work fine for spackling small holes and cracks. Have a hawk and trowel for patching bigger cracks and holes and for larger wall texturing or smoothing patching jobs.

Keep in mind that spackle can take a long time to dry hard in deep or large cracks and holes. A fan or heat lamp can speed things up. In smaller holes, spackle will dry quite fast, especially in hot, dry conditions. It is not recommended to use spackle on very large or deep cracks or holes. *See also* **Holes, Cracks, Prep work, Plastering, Caulking,** and **Quick-setting patching plaster.**

Spar varnishes were once used almost exclusively on the masts of ships, hence their name. Spar varnishes are clear marine varnishes, usually oil-based and either gloss or high-gloss. They are tough, durable clear coatings and can be used outdoors and near water, under adverse conditions.

Specifications: Architectural specifications are put out by certain paint companies to explain their own products. The information can be useful in determining how to use these products properly.

Federal specifications are the grouping and coding of paints according to government standards. You must be familiar with them in order to bid on government jobs.

Speckling is when little drops of paint shoot out of a spray gun instead of a fine mist. It is undesirable when it results from a clogged or defective tip on your spray gun. Clean it or replace it. *See* **Spraying.**

Speckling, or "fly-specks," can be a desired effect when antiquing furniture. You create the effect by dipping a toothbrush into a darker stain and raking your thumb across the bristles. A little goes a long way.

Spinner: a tool for helping to clean rollers or brushes. First, soak and clean your roller cover or brush in water or thinner. Then, snap them to the spinner; by a pump-action, the roller cover or brush spins around, getting rid of most of the paint water or thinners. Spinners speed up your cleaning time. An empty 5-gallon can is a good place to spin out a brush or roller. If you're painting full-time, get a spinner and lubricate it regularly.

Splatter textures are the small, flattened semi-circular drip-like textures found mostly on newer interior ceilings and walls. Splatter textures can be put on in three ways. First there's a special spray rig that sprays out a splatter texture and is used on big splatter-texture jobs. Second, there is a hand-held splatter tool that is loaded first with drywall mud or similar compounds. Then by turning the handle like a jack-in-the-box wind-up toy, splatter texture sprays out on the wall or surface. Third, there is a hand-held, pump-action splatter gun that you load with a liquified texture material sold with the gun. Then by activating the pump, the texture is sprayed onto the surface it is pointed toward. This pump-action gun is recommended for small splatter-texture jobs.

Split coat is an intermediate coat of paint applied between an undercoat and a finish coat on new construction, enamel-finish work. A split coat is composed of a 50/50 mixture of both. Make sure your undercoater and finish paint are chemically compatible before mixing a split coat from them.

Spot-priming is preliminary to touch-up work. Whenever you are touching up problem areas, make sure that you start from the beginning, because no paint will look good over a badly prepared surface. Do all the necessary prep work, no matter how small the scale, and then spot-prime before painting.

Spray cans are effective for small areas and the application of specialty paints only, because they're expensive. Apply spray-can paints in well-ventilated areas and wear an organic vapor respirator, not just a particle mask (*see* **Masks**).

Practice first on a small, unnoticeable area or on a piece of cardboard. This way you can get your technique going. Shake a spray paint can at least sixty to ninety seconds before you start spraying. Shake it from time to time while you are spraying, too, for best results. Hold the spray can from 10 to 15 inches away from the surface and spray on light, even coats, moving the can back and forth. Overlap your strokes slightly and release the spray button at the end of each stroke.

It is recommended to apply two or three thin coats, instead of one thick coat, to prevent drips, sags, or an orange-peel texture from forming.

Don't smoke when spraying with a spray can. And never leave a spray can near a heater, flame or in the sunlight. Don't puncture a spray can and don't attempt to declog the tip of a spray can while it is still attached to the can. Don't throw away a spray can in a garbage compactor and never spray below 66 degrees for best results.

To clear a spray can or prevent it from clogging after you're through painting with it, turn the can upside down and spray until only clear vapors or gas comes out. Next, turn the can right side up and turn the spray head one-quarter inch and then clean the tip with a clean rag. If this method fails to do the trick, then take the spray tip off the can and soak it in lacquer thinner. If this doesn't work, you may have

a bad spray can that needs replacing.

Spray cans contain various colors, enamels, clear finishes, glosses, flats, undercoaters, and primers and can be used on almost any prepped out and cleaned surface. It is a good idea to have a spray can of a quick-drying stain killer. Also, have on hand spray cans containing black and white enamel paints. These spray cans will come in handy from time to time for quickly sealing stains, for fast touch-ups, and for use on small objects, address numbers, and the like.

Spray cans equipped with fan-spray heads are recommended for good spraying results. There are spray-handle tools available at some paint stores that are designed exclusively for using with spray-can paints. They have a trigger release, are easy on your fingers, and are inexpensive.

Spraying: Airless spraying is the recommended method for most paint spraying. Air compressors work well for car finishes, but they waste a lot of paint in overspray. Cup guns, which are connected by a hose to a compressor, work well on fences, furniture, and other small jobs. A

A two- or three-hour brush job can sometimes be done in fifteen minutes using an airless sprayer. Note protection, consisting of spray sock, goggles, and respirator.

cup gun is a cuplike, hand-held container (holding up to a gallon of paint) with a nozzle that sprays out the paint.

A two- or three-hour brush job can sometimes be done by spraying in fifteen to twenty minutes! Whenever feasible, it's best to spray. Louvers, wicker furniture, trellises, large areas, ceilings, walls, and overhangs are all candidates for spray-painting. However, for primer and undercoater paint coats, spraying should be followed by a roller and brush set-up to ensure that the material is worked into the surface well. For efficiency, this is done by another person, who follows behind the person spraying.

Always strain paint to be used for spraying. Make sure the 5-gallon bucket or spray-paint containers are clean and dust-free. Failure to strain paints can cause a tip or filter to clog up, sacrificing time and money. A "pump sock" mesh filter wrapped around your pump filter will prevent clogging. Consider using reversible declogging spray tips, sometimes called "flip-tips."

Don't thin a paint for spraying more than 10 percent by volume. The paint must be thin enough to be sprayed, but thick enough to adhere to the surface without dripping or sagging.

Too much air pressure can sometimes cause a dry and overly fine spray pattern. Too little air pressure can sometimes cause drips, splatters, or a speckled pattern.

It is very important when spraying to mask-off well, and lay down plastic and cloth drops to keep overspray away from things you don't want it on. Also, remember to move cars and to warn people nearby. Don't spray outdoors in gusty or windy weather.

Always wear an organic vapor respirator, not just a dust mask, when spraying (see **Masks**) because overspray contains toxic vapors as well as paint particles. Also, wear a spray hood, gloves, and goggles. Apply petroleum jelly or protective skin lotion to bare skin.

Keep a spray gun 8 inches to 10 inch-

es away from the surface you're spraying. Keep the gun pointed straight at the surface to be sprayed; don't arc a spray gun, as this will cause 40 percent to 60 percent of the paint spray to be wasted as overspray. Less than 10 percent waste is normal. Also don't spray with the gun tilted up or down; this can cause drips or sags. Have a somewhat stiff wrist, always with the gun at 90 degrees to the surface. Lap over each last stroke by 45 percent to 55 percent to prevent a streaky uneven spray pattern. Spray with a regular rhythm. Don't reach or spray farther than is comfortable. Consider using a spray-gun extension pole.

Enamels or clear coatings can be sprayed well following this regimen: First, apply a thin, light spray coat, called a tack-coat. When this tack-coat "flashes," or begins to set up, usually in two to ten minutes, it is ready for step two: Spray a thicker coat, called a wet-coat. A tack coat allows a wet-coat to adhere better, without sagging or dripping. Third, spray on a mist- or fog-coat, if needed for final feathering into a uniform surface. This final coat is thin and light, usually applied at low-pressure.

Spray a room in the following order: First do the corners, then edges followed by protrusions. Then spray the large, flat areas.

Spray shields are handy tools that should not be confused with paint shields. They're from 18 inches to 36 inches long, include a handle, and can be positioned temporarily with one hand while spraying with the other. The store-bought aluminum ones work best, but there are also disposable cardboard shields that fit into inexpensive plastic spray handles, or you can make one yourself out of plywood or cardboard. Don't forget to wash or wipe down your metal spray shield from time to time when spraying, so that drips and caked-up paint don't hinder its effectiveness.

Don't spray bleach through a spray gun, as the latter may be damaged. And to be on the safe side, don't spray anything except paints that say they can be sprayed through an airless sprayer, which includes most paints used today.

There are airless sprayers that can be rented or bought that have two guns and hoses so that two people can use the same machine at the same time.

Clean a spray rig, handle, tip, and filters following each use. Remember to change the oil and lubricate a spray rig from time to time and to do the necessary preventive maintenance.

After using water-based paints, remove the tip and pump out all the remaining paint into its original container. Fill a 5-gallon can with water and begin running it through the apparatus. Paint will come through first, and you can save some of that. Then paint-muddied water will start to flow out. Continue running water until you no longer see any paint in the water.

Next, run some mineral spirits through the hoses and system until you can see only clean mineral spirits. Run some lacquer thinner through the system and lines if you think the airless sprayer needs additional cleaning. Leave the clean mineral spirits in the hose and system until the next use, or run some clean water through. Don't leave lacquer thinner in an airless sprayer overnight.

After using oil-based paints, do the same steps, except don't use the water and run lacquer thinner through your system before using mineral spirits.

Remember never to remove a spray hose from a spray gun without first releasing the fluid pressure. Before removing a spray tip, relieve the fluid pressure and set the safety lock.

Lacquer thinner is a recommended hot solvent to use for cleaning airless sprayer's internal parts and exterior parts, and for cleaning or declogging spray tips. Lacquer thinner also works well on removing unwanted dried or semidry paint overspray on areas, surfaces, and objects.

Don't use wire or a knife to clean or declog a spray tip. A broom straw or a wire tooth brush spray tool can be used to declog a spray tip. *See also* **Electrostatic spray-painting** and **Spray cans.**

Spray tips are numbered usually by how many millimeters wide their hole opening is; different sizes are used for different thicknesses of paints. The tip determines the size and shape of the spray fan. Some suggested spray-tip sizes are .011–.013 for oil-based enamel paints and clear coatings, .015–.019 for thicker vinyl, acrylic, or latex-based flat paints. Enamels and clear coatings will spray out well from a tip smaller than that used for water-based flat paints. Many latex, acrylic, or vinyl flat paints will not spray out of tips that are usually used for enamels or clear coatings. When in doubt as to which spray tip to use, consult the manager of the paint store where you bought the paint. Tungsten carbide is a good material for use in making spray tips.

There are self-cleaning airless spray tips available that will clear a clog without having to be removed. These turn-around, reversible self-cleaning, or flip-tips, work well for most airless spraying. Always strain your paints and have clean containers so that a spray tip doesn't become unnecessarily clogged. Generally speaking, most spray problems involve a spray-tip problem of some sort. Spray tips can be cleaned with a painter's toothbrush, a small wire brush resembling a toothbrush, or with a broom straw. Don't use a metal wire thicker than the metal bristle found on a wire brush to clean a spray tip. Lacquer thinner is the best solvent to soak or clean spray tips with.

Stain-killer sealer refers to any good-quality primer, usually oil-based, that will seal against bleed-through, as from previously water-damaged areas, scuff marks or plaster patches. White shellac often serves as a stain killer. *See also* **Under-coaters.**

Stainless steel: Don't paint over stain-less steel if at all possible. Paint does not adhere well to stainless steel.

Stains are basically thin paints, ranging from transparent to solid-body. They pen-etrate wood to color it and, to a lesser degree than other paints, to protect it. They are usually used alone on decks, shingles, and outdoor furniture; on interi-or woodwork they are more often used in conjunction with clear coatings.

Remember stains need to penetrate, so don't use them over enamels or flat paints. However, a solid-body stain can cover a previously applied solid-body stain, and a semi-transparent stain can cover a previously applied semi-transpar-ent stain.

For durability stains are not recom-mended for use on exterior doors, win-dows, fascia boards, or trimwork where these are subject to direct sunlight. Con-sider using an enamel paint instead for greater protection. Semi-transparent stains will weather faster than solid-body stains. If you use semi-transparent stains as your only coating on bare, exposed wood areas that weather quickly, then consider restaining at the first sign of weathering.

Cedar takes to stains more quickly than most other woods, such as pine, cypress and other sappy woods. Soft-woods can soak up additional color, and can become darker than hardwoods when the same kind and color of semi-transparent stain is applied. There are available pre-stain wood conditioners that are specially formulated to help pine, spruce, fir, and other softwoods absorb semi-transparent stains more evenly. Pre-stain wood conditioners should be used first to help achieve a more uniform look on two different species of wood that will receive the same color of semi-transpar-ent stain.

A bad stain job, one that is streaky, thick, or too dark, can usually be fixed by bleaching, thoroughly rinsing, and then re-staining.

Except for refinishing work or small amounts of interior trim, stain can be applied with good results by airless spraying, followed by someone with a roller and brush set-up to work the wet stain into the surface and correct drips and holidays. Use this method on exteri-ors, large areas, and where wiping off is not necessary. Rolling solid-body stains is a good method for applying them, along with a brush cut-in set-up, if spraying is not wanted or practical. Consider using a rough-rider staining tool when applying stains.

Using a semi-transparent stain with a brush and wiping it off with a rag or applying it by rag only is relatively easy to do. The main thing to remember is: Create an even, uniform look throughout the surface. Generally speaking, 20 per-cent to 50 percent of a semi-transparent stain after it has been applied is wiped off by rags.

It is important to mix in all the pig-ments and paint materials on the bottom of a stain can (*see* **Boxing** paints). Don't play chemist and try to invent a stain from an oil- or water-based pigmented paint by thinning it way down.

A semi-transparent stain can be used with an oil-based clear finish in a mixture, but don't use more than 14 ounces of stain to one gallon clear coating for best results.

Don't put a semi-transparent or solid-body stain over a clear coating and avoid using stains on bricks, masonry, stucco, concrete, plaster, or any metal surface. It is not a good idea to use stains as under-coaters for enamel- or flat-finish paints.

Mineral spirits can be used to thin or lighten the color on an oil-based semi-transparent stain, but don't use more than 45 percent mineral spirits to stain.

Solid-body stains are similar to thinned-down wall paints. They can cover in much the same way as wall paint on wood, but they do not completely hide the grain. They can be used on bare wood, whereas a flat wall paint is not recommended as a first paint coat on a bare wood surface.

Water-based solid-body stains are easy to use. They cover nicely, don't have an unpleasant odor, and leave few or no lap marks, so they can be applied rather rapidly. They clean up easily with water. They are usually made from latex or acrylic resins. They are good to use when breaking in an inexperienced painter

Solid-body latex or acrylic solid-body water-based stains are longer lasting and keep their color longer than semi-transparent stains when they are used as a finish coat of paint on an exterior surface.

After letting a semi-transparent stain dry thoroughly, fill in holes with putty of the correct tint. *See* **Putty.** However, the order is a personal choice, as the reverse is done by many people. There are available at some paint stores pencil-like products that come in different tints that can be used in place of putty for filling in countersunk nail holes on interior wooden refinishing surfaces. *See* **Woods, Bleach, Brushing, Rolling, Spraying, Paint,** and **Drying times.**

Steel wool finds several uses in the painting world: coarse steel wool removes chipped paint; finer steel wools smooth or burnish surfaces after sanding. Fine steel wool also works well for blending touched-up spots into a surface.

Stipple is a texture that's left usually by a medium to rough roller nap, or it can be made by a stipple texture gun or tool. There are available stipple texture roller covers that resemble carpeting; they can be used to produce a medium to heavy stipple texture on a ceiling or a wall. A stipple texture is not a splatter texture.

Stir sticks and mixing paddles are necessary tools for painting jobs and, accompanied by a purchase, are usually given away free by paint dealers. Consider drilling a $1/4$-inch hole $3/4$ inch from the bottom of a stir stick to help give a better flow and stir to it.

Strainers can be made of cheese cloth, nylon, or paper. They can usually be bought in one-, two-, or five-gallon sizes. You can also make your own strainers from pantyhose or stockings. Strain any and all paints before using them for spraying. Enamels and most clear coatings benefit from being strained. It improves brushing and helps prevent color tints from streaking later. Take a look at the stuff the strainer catches in some paints to see for yourself what a good idea straining paint is!

Stripper: *See* **Paint remover.**

Stucco is loosely defined as porous sandy concrete or plaster that usually contains cement, lime, sand and water. To patch stucco surfaces, determine the sand-grit size that is used on the particular surface to be patched. Is it 16-, 30-, or 60-grit silica sand, or is it a rougher plaster sand?

For large stucco painting jobs, mix together roughly one part plastic cement to two parts sand, or use more sand if a rougher texture is desired. Mix in some plaster glue for added bonding strength. Use a hawk, trowel, and float or stiff-bristled brush for patching stucco holes and cracks.

Use premixed dry-stucco patching-bag mixes for small holes and cracks in stucco surfaces, provided the grit size matches.

Remember to moisten a prepped hole or crack prior to applying stucco-patching mixes for a lasting bond and best results.

When repairing stucco, you need stucco patch, plaster glue, cloth gloves, and the following tools: (back) trowel, hock; (front) float and 5-inch broad-knife.

Sometimes a finished patch needs to be moistened from time to time during curing so it won't dry too fast and crack.

Very porous stucco should be watered down well one night prior to painting. Make sure the surface is not wet, but just a little damp, before painting.

Before painting over prepainted stucco surfaces it is a good idea to use a wire brush (with a bit of elbow grease) to put tooth in the stucco for a better paint bond.

Some blown-on unpainted stucco surfaces should be tested first with wet paint in a small inconspicuous place to see if it will flash, or develop an inconsistent sheen in reaction to the stucco.

Exterior water-based flat masonry paints are good finishes for stucco surfaces. Keep in mind that unless they are chalky, masonry surfaces don't require an undercoater if a good-quality latex or acrylic water-based flat masonry paint is used.

Spraying stucco surfaces with an airless sprayer, followed by a person with a roller set-up is a good, fast painting method. When rolling porous stucco surfaces, a roller nap of 1$\frac{1}{4}$ inches to 1$\frac{1}{2}$ inches is recommended. *See also* **Masonry, Plaster, Sand, Glue, Holes, Cracks, Hawk, Trowel, Float,** and **Paint.**

Surface bonder is a clear or amber solution that is added to a paint or undercoater to improve its adhesiveness on chalky surfaces. A surface bonder mixed with a water-based solid-body stain that says on its label it can be used on masonry surfaces makes a good, versatile, inexpensive undercoater.

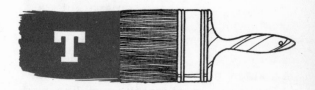

Tack rags are specially made sticky rags used mostly on quality trim work and furniture refinishing. They pick up dust, lint, and particles and are usually flame-resistant, and can stay somewhat tacky for a long time. Most paint stores carry tack rags, but with a clean rag and a little varnish or drying oil and turpentine you can make your own version of a tack rag. A little turpentine, water, or a clear finish can sometimes bring back to life a dried-out tack rag.

Texture coatings are special plasterlike coatings that are usually sprayed on the entire exterior of a house or building with the exception of the doors and windows. They are expensive and have been marketed as highly successful coatings. In reality they still need more perfecting. They are a matter of personal choice, especially where looks are concerned, and no recommendations are given for them at this time. They can be repainted over.

Texture paints can be rolled or brushed on. Don't use an airless paint sprayer. There are different kinds of texture paints for different kinds of surfaces. Texture paints can cover many flaws such as small cracks, bumps, and missed texture and pattern areas. There are also texture additives that prevent skidding and slipping on slick wet floors when they are added to the finish coats.

Texture paints come ready-made and in powdered form. Read the label of a texture paint to see if it can be used outdoors before using it on an exterior area or surface. Also, remember: Texture paints are hard to remove and smooth over once they have bonded and dried hard.

Thinners: Mineral spirits, turpentine, kerosene, naphtha, lacquer thinner, and even water are all "thinners." Fast-drying thinners include lacquer thinner and naphtha; kerosene is a slow-drying thinner. The main purpose of thinners is to reduce the thickness of paints. Thinners also help ease of operation, leveling, adhesiveness, and the consistency of paints. And of course thinners are essential for cleaning up paints.

Almost all paints require some thinning during a painting operation. The snag and gluey characteristics of unthinned paints are not to be desired. However, over-thinning a paint will result in less film thickness and runny, drippy work.

Have a light hand when thinning paints. Don't thin lacquer-based paints with mineral spirits. However, some oil-based paints can be thinned with lacquer thinners for faster drying times. Never thin oil-based paints with water or reduce water-based paints with thinners that are used for oil-based paints. The wrong thinners in a coating can wreak havoc.

Special manufactured packaged thinners designed for oil-based paints and others that are designed for water-based paints are usually good products to use to thin paints. They do cost more per gallon, however, than bulk mineral spirits and clean water.

Use rubber gloves when cleaning with thinners other than water. Use body lotion, Vaseline gels, or suntan oils to restore skin that has dried out from exposure to mineral spirits or similar thinners.

Generally speaking, it is a good idea to buy 50 percent or 100 percent more of a thinning agent than what you think you'll need for a particular painting job. Consider economizing on mineral spirits by storing used dirty thinners in a clean container, such as a glass milk jug. After three weeks or so, there will be clean thinner on the top and settled junk on the bottom. Slowly pour out the clean thinner into an appropriate container for future use and throw away the settled junk.

Don't use thinners other than water to remove paint from porcelain or marble tile. *See also* **Mineral spirits, Lacquer, Naphtha, Turpentine,** and **Reducers.**

Thresholds get walked on a lot and in entryways are exposed to the elements. Use a durable high gloss enamel or, if you want to see wood grain, a polyurethane varnish on a wood threshold. It is a good idea to leave a metal threshold bare, or use a metal undercoater on it and then finish-paint it with an exterior high gloss enamel for greater durability. Don't forget to put a "Wet Paint" sign in front of a newly painted threshold!

Tile: It is advisable not to paint tile. And avoid accidentally spilling paint or harsh cleaning solutions on expensive tile floors. A linoleum floor, however, can be painted over with a labeled floor enamel or clear finish, or it can be finished with an appropriate wax. Vinyl or rubber tile floors should have only appropriate waxes put on them but no paints. Ceramic tiles might get a silicone sealer, more to protect the grout than for the tile.

Titanium dioxide is an extremely dense, white pigment with excellent hiding properties that is used in paints and undercoaters, especially stain killers.

Tools and gear: Here is a quick list, essential to a professional, but no less useful to anyone tackling a paint job around the house: brushes, drops, ladders, knives, caulking gun and tubes, spackle, roller set-up, roller pole, buckets, rags, sandpaper, duster brush, wire brush, scraper, razor blades, masking tape, broom, hammer, stir sticks, T.S.P., sponge, putty, goggles, particle mask, paint thinner, hand cream, undercoaters, finish paints, and painting clothes and shoes.

More prep tools: Back row: tack rag. Next row L to R: pot hook, stir stick. Next row L to R: wire brush, triangular molding scraper, medium-size square scraper, wallpaper scrapers. Front row L to R: 4" flat-broad-knife, 5" flat broad-knife, standard size putty knife, and particle, or dust, mask.

Tooth refers to a slightly rough texture that is ideal for paint to adhere to. Roughing a glossy surface with sandpaper or etching a metal one with acid gives the surface "tooth."

Traffic paints are used on asphalt or concrete surfaces for traffic control. Some come in reflector coatings for night visibility. Traffic paints give good coverage to the gallon and are extremely weather- and wear-resistant. If you want to build your own parking lot or outdoor basketball court, consider using traffic paint.

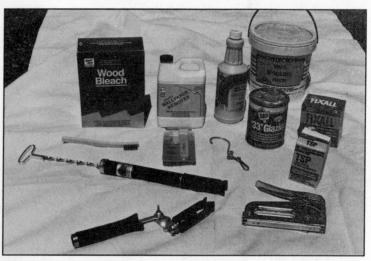

These tools and materials are useful for getting surfaces ready to paint: Back row L to R: wood bleach, wallpaper remover, water-base paint thinner, spackle. Next row L to R: wire brush, brush comb, pot-hook, window glazing compound, quick-patch. Next row L to R: airless-sprayer, TSP. Front row L to R: extend-a-tool and power staple gun.

Trays: Rolling out of a 5-gallon container with a 9-inch screen for large areas or a 2-gallon container with a 7-inch screen for smaller areas is recommended instead of working out of a paint tray. However, in very small or cramped spaces trays are worthwhile. Paint trays come in steel, aluminum, and plastic. Paint-tray liners are inexpensive and smart to use, making clean-up easy. A grid or a screen can be used in a paint tray, but it is not necessary.

Fill a paint tray only up to where the corrugations begin. Roll into the deep end of the paint, submerging the roller about half way, then roll it back and forth on the corrugations, covering the rest of the roller cover uniformly. Next, twirl your roller slowly in the air to the surface you're rolling. The twirling helps prevent paint dripping from the roller as it's transported to the surface from the tray.

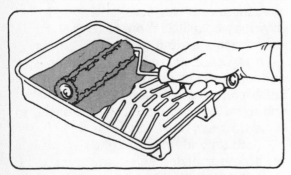

Correct paint amount for paint tray

Always remove all paint from a tray after using it and a clean it well. Failure to do so will result in paint build-up. Whenever you clean up a steel paint tray with water, make sure you wipe it completely dry, so that rust doesn't form.

Trellis: Airless sprayers and cup guns work well for finish-painting a trellis.

T.S.P. is trisodium phosphate. It is a detergent sold in supermarkets and paint-supply stores. It is in the form of saltlike crystals that dissolve in water. The water becomes slippery and will wet a surface more thoroughly.

T.S.P. is moderately toxic to breathe and to the skin. Wear rubber gloves when using it and rinse skin that comes in contact with it.

Eight to ten ounces of T.S.P. added to one gallon of water will help dull the gloss of many surfaces. Four to six ounces of T.S.P. to one gallon of water will remove slight and minor cases of mildew. A strong solution of T.S.P. and water can be used to take wallpaper glue off walls. Tobacco stains, soot, dirt, pollution, grime, and the like can be washed and cleaned with a strong T.S.P. solution.

It is a good idea to start washing at the bottom of work upward to prevent permanent streaking and staining from occurring below. Avoid getting T.S.P. on any surfaces that are not to be painted, as the T.S.P. solution can be harmful. Ceramic, marble, porcelain tiles and surfaces, and clear finishes should not come in contact with T.S.P. solutions.

Tung oil, also called China wood oil, is a yellow or brownish drying oil that comes from the tung tree. It is a high-quality ingredient found in many paints and varnishes.

Pure tung oil leaves a rather dull gloss. Several manufacturers make a tung-oil finish which is basically a varnish, in that it includes resins and driers, and the tung oil has been heat-treated to speed polymerization. It does penetrate bare wood, and it is usually brushed or wiped on with a rag and then wiped off. The more coats, the more the finish builds up on the surface, providing more protection and more gloss.

Turpentine is a thin volatile oil made from pine trees. It is used as a thinner for oil-based paints. There are basically two grades: Gum turpentine, which is the more expensive, is made by distilling pine sap and is used mainly by artists; and steam-distilled or wood turpentine, which comes from pine stumps and scraps, is fine for paint jobs. Turpentine has a pronounced, though not unpleasant odor. It is nevertheless moderately toxic to breathe and allergenic, especially after long exposure. Turpentine has largely been replaced by mineral spirits, which is less odorous and less expensive.

Undercoaters, also called primers, are designed to adhere well to bare surfaces and provide a good ground for applying top coats.

As prep work is so important to a painting finish, so too is a good-quality undercoater. One of the most common painting mistakes that produces inferior, unprofessional, nondurable painting jobs is the failure to use the right high-quality undercoater or primer before the finish-paint coats are applied.

Sealers can be used like undercoaters, but they are not identical. Sealers do not penetrate as well as undercoaters. Their principal function is to seal the surface, not necessarily provide the best ground for painting over. New interior drywall is often sealed with water-based wall sealers or PVA sealers.

There are also fast-drying stain-killer sealers that are great for preventing bleed-through. Some stain-killer sealers can be used to fill in hairline cracks. Don't use stain-killer sealers on metal surfaces subject to high temperatures. Except for preventing bleed-through, stain-killer sealers should not be used for priming bare exterior surfaces in place of an appropriate exterior undercoater. Don't apply a stain-killer below 55 degrees.

It is recommended that an undercoater precede a pigmented top coat on the following surfaces: any glossy surface, any bare surface receiving a finish flat or enamel paint, any surface where a flat or enamel finish paint is going to be covering over a semi-transparent stain, and any patched surface.

On high-gloss surfaces, where a lesser gloss or dead flat finish is going over it, stronger bonding synthetic undercoaters are available. However, these are expensive.

Oil-based undercoaters, with their typically good penetration, are durable, resist cracking and chipping, and do not raise the grain of woods. Water-based undercoaters can raise the grain on bare wood surfaces. But their advantages include being faster drying and nonodorous.

Don't thin water-based undercoaters unless it is absolutely necessary. Don't use an interior undercoater on an exterior surface. Exterior undercoaters can be used on interior surfaces, however, but they may be a little more toxic than similar interior ones and take longer to dry.

It is a good idea to always tint an undercoater a little bit lighter than the finish-paint coats. The finish-paint coats will cover it better, and it will be easier to avoid holidays (missed spots).

Sand an undercoater lightly when it is dry before applying an enamel over it.

In areas of high humidity or moisture, use two coats of an undercoater on bare surfaces, especially metal ones.

Always paint over an undercoater before twelve days have gone by to prevent peeling or flaking.

Make sure that you let any undercoater dry for at least 10 percent longer than the longest drying time given on the label. It is important that an undercoater or primer is completely dry before other paint coats go on top of it; otherwise, the top coat can lift and wrinkle. *See also* **Enamels, Masonry conditioner, Metal, Paint, Prep work, Sanding sealer, Shellac, Stain-killer sealer, Surface bonder,** and **Wood.**

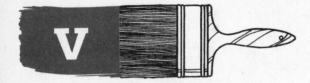

Varnish can be resins dissolved in solvents that dry simply by the evaporation of the solvent (like shellac) or resins cooked with oil that dry by both evaporation and polymerization (like copal/linseed oil varnish). Varnishes can be largely synthetic (like polyurethane), and they can even be made at home simply by wrapping a resin in cheesecloth and suspending it in a solvent overnight. Varnish dries to a clear or translucent film.

Varnishes come in many different glosses, from matte to high gloss, and everything in between. Check your paint dealer's clear-coated wood samples to determine which gloss you want. Tint varnishes only with oil-based color tints or with oil-based semi-transparent stains.

For tougher resistance to chemicals or abrasion, use a polyurethane or epoxy varnish. Use a marine spar varnish where there's direct sunlight or moisture and where a natural look and a clear varnish are desired on an exterior surface. Most other varnishes are not recommended for exterior use.

Alkyd sanding sealers are recommended as the base coat on interior bare wooden surfaces when a alkyd varnish is going to be the top coat.

Varnishes can be thinned with mineral spirits, turpentine, and other similar types of packaged thinners. Some thinning of varnishes is sometimes needed to achieve better leveling and flow. However, never overthin a varnish.

Spraying or brushing are recommended as the methods for applying varnishes. For best results use natural brushes instead of synthetic bristle brushes. Rolling may be used for applying varnish to a floor, but it is not recommended for most other work. If you must use a roller, use a short-nap cover and try not to leave obvious roller stipple marks. Use two or three thin coats of varnish instead of one thick coat.

Varnish finishes that have cracked or been scratched usually cannot be touched-up without showing lap marks. They must be completely sanded or prepped and then varnished over.

Maintain a wet edge when applying varnishes and always work from a dry area to your last wet-edge area. Don't stop in the middle of varnishing. Instead, complete a side, entire area, or object before stopping or squaring-up.

It is a good idea to recoat varnish surfaces when they are scratched or you can see the start of hairline cracks. At this stage, a good sanding job and two or three finish coats of varnish should be sufficient for repainting and maintenance painting. *See also* **Clear coatings, Brushes, Spraying, Woods, Metals,** and **Paint.**

Vinegar is a mild acid and can be used to treat efflorescence, or alkali deposits on masonry. Unthinned vinegar can also be used to treat new galvanized metals. Always rinse thoroughly with water any surface or area on which vinegar has been used.

Vinyl is a clear, synthetic resin. Most vinyl paints are water-based paints and have little or no gloss. Except for those formulated for marine environments, they are not to be preferred over similar premium-grade acrylic, alkyd, or latex paints. However, combination formulas, like vinyl-acrylic interior wall primer, can be quite good. *See* **Paint.**

Viscosity is the degree to which paints resist flow under an applied force such as brushing, rolling, spraying, or pouring.

Wallpaper: It is not recommended to paint over wallpaper. But if you do decide to paint over wallpaper, make sure the wallpaper is glued down securely everywhere, especially at corners and edges. Next, test a small area and see how the paint and wallpaper react and dry out together. If the pattern shows through, it may be a good idea to remove the wallpaper for best results. If it must be painted over, put a stain killer or a shellac primer over it before any finish-paint coats are applied. Burlap and grass cloth wallpapers may need three or four coats of finish paint on them for best results. Remember that it is harder to remove wallpaper that has already been painted over. Steamers or liquid wallpaper removers will not easily saturate it.

Wallpaper can be removed by a wallpaper steamer, sometimes called an "iron," which can be rented from paint or rental stores. These steamers work quite well. Another method is to use commercial liquid wallpaper remover or a strong concentrated dish soap and water mixture. Apply the solution by roller or garden sprayer. Let it soak for a while, apply it again, and then remove it with a wallpaper scraper, broad knife, or similar tool. The secret to this method is to soak and saturate the wallpaper thoroughly. Always keep an area of wallpaper soaking ahead of the wallpaper you're currently scraping off.

Most hung wallpaper is backed with a brownish paper that must be removed. The more glue that was originally used on this paper backing the more trouble it is to remove. Use a strong T.S.P. and water solution after the wallpaper is removed to clean the walls of glue, size, paste, and so forth. Warm water and detergent in a strong mixture can also be used. Keep water off the electrical wall

outlets and switches for obvious safety reasons.

Spackle is an excellent filler to use to patch holes, cracks, chips and tears after wallpaper removal.

Wallpapering: Learning how to hang wallpaper is a good second trade for a full-time painter to learn. Most paper-hanging is done as piece-work: a set price per hung roll of wallpaper.

An easy way to estimate the number of rolls of wallpaper to be used on a wallpapering job is to figure out the square footage of all the wall areas to be papered, subtract from this number door and window areas and divide by the square footage of the particular wallpaper roll, which is usually 36 square feet if the roll is made in the U. S. Add in a waste factor—typically 3 to 6 square feet per roll, depending on the pattern, the person hanging it and the particular job conditions.

The primary tools needed during a wallpapering operation include the following: broad knife, paste brush, drops, stepladder, paste table, smoothing rollers, razor blades, smoothing brushes, a good-sized straightedge, special wallpapering shears, a clean fiver, and sponges.

First is prep work: Dust, dirt, and grime must be removed; cracks and holes must be filled. Don't wallpaper over a glossy wall. Instead, break the gloss with a light sanding and then size it. Size is basically glue allowed to dry on a surface to seal and somewhat fill the pores. Bare plaster areas, and any patched areas, should be sized before wallpapering for best results. A paper lining may first be needed on a wall or ceiling prior to the finish roll of wallpaper on it. Paper linings help adhesion; they help achieve smoother seams; and they help avoid bubbles and wrinkles.

Always have good lighting when wallpapering.

It's best to have more than enough of a patterned wallpaper on hand. If you don't you may have trouble getting an exact match in the next run of it. Also, dye lots differ. Always check your rolls before beginning, in the same way you would check a custom color paint before applying it

Measure out and add on a couple of inches or more to your strips before cutting them.

The drying-out of wallpaper prematurely after it has been pasted and before it is hung up is one of the main problems to learn how to overcome. Air drafts and hot weather dry out exposed wallpaper paste on wallpaper fast. Learn to work fast. After pasting, folding the paper (not creasing it) can slow the paste's drying. Always paper the ceiling first before you do the walls in a room.

Start in the middle areas of a particular wallpaper strip when pasting it up and then work toward the edges. Have a light hand when pasting wallpaper, especially toward the edges, to avoid getting any wallpaper paste on the front side.

Wall areas with a window or windows are good places to start papering. The most unnoticed area or place in a particular room is a good place to finish up. The first strip of wallpaper hung on a particular ceiling or wall is the most important one, because all the other strips to follow have the first strip as their guide. Consider snapping a chalkline to achieve a straight, true line against which to lay flush your first strip of wallpaper.

When gently smoothing out a particular piece of paper on a wall or ceiling, work from the middle to the edges, getting rid of all wrinkles, ridges and bubbles. Double check all border areas of a wallpaper strip after you have hung it to make sure they are down firm with no gaps.

At corners, wrap around only ¼ inch; this avoids both wrinkles and unsightly seams.

Excess paste on any unwanted areas should be removed with a moist sponge before it hardens and is a chore to get off. To help achieve a first-rate wallpaper job, run a seam roller gently along the joints, unless your paper is flocked or embossed. Do this when the wallpaper paste has tacked-up but not completely dried.

Wallpaper scraper: A razor-like blade tool that is good to have on most painting jobs for scraping windows clean of paint drips and overspray. It has many other uses, including removing wallpaper.

Warming paints: The recommendation is not to heat up paints unless it is absolutely necessary. Warming up paints is an alternative method for keeping painting going right along when temperatures start to go below 50 degrees. Paints can be warmed by wrapping them in electric blankets or by putting them in hot water with the lid off the can or simply by putting them in a warmer room. Never heat oil- or water-based paints over or close to an open or exposed flame or fire.

Some airless sprayers can be equipped with hoses and certain kinds of machinery that can warm paint up before it is ejected. The paint sprays out drier and there is little or no thinning needed. Some paints and undercoaters, however, don't respond well to this type of warming and can become inconsistent. On very cold surfaces or on wet or damp surfaces, warming the paint is no cure at all.

Warranties and guarantees: If you are a full-time painter, you should give a guarantee to your work. If you ever have to go back and redo work, be assured you are not the first person that has had to do so. The best professional painters have had to go back and fix work at one time or another. However, get to the point where you don't have to go back because you have gone over everything well before completing the job.

If you are having your house or business painted by a professional, get some kind of guarantee. Generally speaking, quality painters and those with reputations for doing good work will give a guarantee, thereby backing up their work.

If you have followed all the directions on a paint-can label, done all the prep work correctly, and applied the undercoaters and finish paints professionally, and yet a paint manufacturer's undercoaters or paints fail, you should be able to recover those losses. However, a manufacturer (or your local paint shop) may check your work for error.

In case of an accident with a ladder or other equipment or tool, if you try to sue the manufacturers they will want to know if you used all of the stated safety precautions and whether you went over the weight limits of their equipment.

Water-based paints or water-emulsion paints are made up of drying oils, pigments, and resins in a water solution. Water-based paints have come a long way since they were first made available.

The advantages of water-based paints are: They are easy to apply. They usually have almost no odor to them. They don't contain mineral spirits or paint thinners. They dry faster than other paints. And they usually clean up using water only. The disadvantages of some water-based paints is that they don't penetrate deeply. Water-based flat paints and water-based masonry paints are somewhat better than similar oil-based ones. Water-based solid-body stains are also usually better paint coatings than similar type oil-based ones. *See also* **Emulsion, Vinyl, Latex, Acrylic,** and **Paint.**

Waterblasting, technically called hydro-blasting, involves a high-pressure water pump. A water hose is hooked up to the water blaster and water is forced out through a long wand that has a spray tip on the end to regulate the shape and size of the water fan. Make sure your water source has enough flow to operate the blaster correctly. Test it by timing how long it takes to fill a 5-gallon bucket and compare this to the recommended rate for the blaster. Make sure your water source is always on when operating the blaster, or you can damage it.

Most waterblasters are gasoline operated, so make sure you use the right kind of gasoline in them. Electric-powered water blasters or spray cleaners are not as powerful or efficient as gasoline-operated ones. Waterblasters can be bought or they can be rented by the hour, day or week, usually at large paint shops and rental yards.

Watch out for slippery work conditions when waterblasting and aim a waterblaster only at the work to be done. Be careful of windows. When waterblasting, use the proper tips; the size depends on the surfaces to be cleaned. Aim the waterblaster at an angle, and it will work more efficiently in removing paint chips, not building materials.

Waterblasters can also be used with add-on attachments, which shoot out sand and water at the same time.

Waterproofing is a way of protecting a surface from water or moisture penetration. Waterproofing done on wooden surfaces can usually help reduce shrinking, swelling, warping, grain raising, and splitting. Waterproofing on masonry surfaces helps slow erosion. Water should bead up on it, although in time, hard rains will penetrate.

Most water-repellent sealers are made with silicone and are colorless, with minimal odor. A good water-repellent sealer should not color the surface to which it is applied. Sometimes it will create a wet look.

The recommendation is to apply a water-repellent sealer liberally and apply two coats instead of one for best results.

Never use a water-repellent sealer on a damp or wet surface. Wait three days or longer after a rain before waterproofing. Also, make sure that the temperature on the surface to be treated is above 45 degrees.

When a natural look is to be desired on a bare wood surface, a water-repellent sealer can be considered as a finish coating. But make sure before applying it over another coat of paint that the label indicates compatibility.

A clean portable garden sprayer with a small storage tank works well for applying water-repellent sealers. However, almost all painting methods can be used as well. *See also* **Paint.**

Water putty is a brownish putty that usually dries rock hard in sixty to eighty minutes. It is used where water or moisture are problems. Water putty when completely hardened can be sawn in two.

Waxes: As a finish by themselves, liquid and paste waxes are not recommended. They are not durable enough. However, as a finishing touch over a clear coating, waxes look nice and add protection. Refinished furniture and wood floors are commonly waxed. Trimwork done in a clear finish can also be waxed. Most commercial waxes are a combination of individual waxes, like carnauba for hardness or beeswax for workability. Wax finishes can usually be cleaned or washed by weak household detergents and then rinsed with water and wiped dry. Mineral spirits also dissolves wax.

Do not paint directly over a waxed or polished surface. Always remove the wax first.

Apply paste wax with a soft cloth, let it form a haze, and buff it off. On rougher, textured, or wood-grained surfaces, a soft brush can be used.

Weather: Paint doesn't work well, adhere well, or dry well when it's too cold, too hot, or too humid, not to mention when it's raining. If you can paint when the weather is pleasant, your job will come out best. For best results, do not paint outside when the temperature is above 95 degrees or below 50 degrees, and avoid painting in high wind or high humidity.

Indoors, normal room temperature is right for painting. And don't forget about proper ventilation.

In temperatures above 85 degrees, you can add kerosene or linseed oil to improve the workability of your oil-based paints. Use lacquer thinner to loosen up sticky brush bristles in hot weather, whether or not you are using oil- or water-based paints. Brush and roller painting work above 85 degrees can begin to be difficult. *See also* **Drying** and **Humidity.**

Weather stripping: Some latex-based paints don't stick well to weather stripping, so consider using another type of paint, such as exterior epoxy paint, that adheres better if you must paint over it.

Whitewashes are made of lime and water or of whiting (calcium carbonate), glue, and water. Whitewashing has been around for a long time. It is an inexpensive way to freshen up a surface; however, I do not recommend using whitewashes. They do not look good and are not durable. They might be fine for a farm outbuilding, but they should not be used on a house or quality commercial building. Today there are whitewashes available for different surfaces. If you want to use a whitewash, it is recommended to dampen the surface area on which it will be applied. As a result, the whitewash should then flow, level-out, and stick better to the surface.

If you mix up whitewash yourself, protect your eyes and skin, as lime paste is caustic and can burn.

Spraying is the fastest and often the best method of applying whitewashes. Make sure you strain whitewash three or more times before spraying it. A roller and brush set-up is a good painting method for applying whitewashes when spraying is not practical or possible. There are special large whitewash brushes available at some paint stores.

Some whitewashes don't respond well to color tints added to them. It is a good idea to try and tint a small amount of whitewash first to see how the color tints react to it.

A whitewash finish cures best in humid, even damp conditions.

Don't paint over a previously painted whitewash-finished surface directly with another kind of finish paint. Instead, remove the chalking on the whitewash surface with an acid solution, 20 percent to 30 percent muriatic acid in water, or use undiluted vinegar and elbow grease. Rinse the surface thoroughly with water and let it dry. Then apply a masonry conditioner or a surface bonder mixed with your paint as a primer coat. After the primer coat has dried completely, apply the finish-paint coats.

Whiting is calcium carbonate, or chalk, used to make putty and glazing compounds when linseed oil is added. Whiting is also used to make a form of Swedish putty when oil-based paints are added to it.

Windows involve careful and sometimes tedious work, both in preparation and in painting. Wallpaper scrapers, razor blades, and a razor-blade scraper tool are all good for scraping dried paint chips and overspray from window panes. Don't apply too much pressure on the glass when scraping windows.

It may be easier to take windows out, code them, and then prep and paint them

To get rid of dried paint on a clear window pane, use either a razor-blade scraper (left) or a wallpaper scraper (right).

on top of sawhorses or against a wall on wooden blocks.

For the cut-in work, you might use masking tape, a paint shield, or liquid

Taping and painting a window

masking tape, but there's no substitute for plain old painting skill in making a window look good.

There are several different styles of window. A casement window is a single framed hinged on the side. Paint the top first, the sides next and the bottom last. A double-hung window consists of two separate windows in adjacent tracks, one in front of the other. Each window can include interior framework separating individual panes of glass. Work from the surfaces farthest away first, from top to bottom. A fixed window is a window that doesn't open. It can include an interior framework, in which case, paint it just as if it's one section of a double-hung window.

Don't flood window jambs with paint. You might not even paint them at all.

Painting double-hung and casement windows

Window sills that constantly have water sitting on them will eventually peel. Keep in mind that paint can drip or build up in the bottom corners of window panes, sills, and ledges. It is a good idea after painting to take a somewhat dry brush and with the tips of the bristles pull out the excess paint in the corners. Don't brush too much paint onto the top rail of a casement or double-hung window, or it will drip over onto the other side.

Leave a window slightly ajar after painting so that it doesn't dry in a shut position. If you think a window will get stuck in place after it dries, move it up and down or in and out from time to time while it is drying. Petroleum jelly used on window edges and corners after they have been painted and tacked-up will reduce their chances of sticking or lifting paint.

If a stuck window must be opened, use a sawtooth blade tool designed for opening stuck windows, or use a putty knife, broad knife, or screwdriver. *See also* **Putty** and **Glazing.**

Wood expands and contracts unevenly as it absorbs and releases moisture. These changes in dimension can cause splitting, warping, and surface-checking. Paint does not fully seal a wood surface, but it does inhibit the exchange of moisture and therefore works to preserve wood.

New wood should be allowed to reach equilibrium moisture content with its surroundings before being painted. If the wood is green, or newly cut, this can take as much as a year per inch of thickness. But more likely the wood has been kiln-dried or is old, in which case a few days of dry weather should do it. Don't paint wood that is wet. Wood to be painted should be clean, dry, and free of fungus or mildew. Paint also looks and works better on wood that has been sanded; outdoors stains are an exception.

If you want a pigmented finish coat, especially an enamel, apply an undercoater first, preferably an oil-based one because it gives grater penetration. Double-coat end grain, whenever you can. Knots, water-damage stains, sap, and potential bleed-through spots should be sealed with an aluminum paint, a shellac primer, or a stain-killer. These problems can be treated with mineral spirits, naphtha, or denatured alcohol, if you're covering with a stain or clear coating. Either of these can be your only finishing material on wood, or you can top a stain with a clear coating, as is usually done on furniture. Outdoors, use a wood preservative for a clear finish. On very porous woods or man-made compositions, such as plywood, particleboard, or flakeboard, apply two coats of a quality exterior wood undercoater before applying a pigmented paint (not a solid-body stain). Semi-transparent stains and clear coatings don't generally work well on man-made boards, unless they are indoors in shops or garages. Wood shingles, two-by-fours, posts, and similar wooden products can have stains or wood preservatives applied by dipping.

Remember that exposed or popped nail heads allow moisture to get inside the wooden surfaces and as a result splitting, cracking, and rust streaks can occur. So countersink popped nails and then caulk or spackle over them. To prevent rust streaks from occurring on wooden surfaces such as shingles and fences, use stainless-steel or aluminum nails on them. If you don't want to remove rusted nails from a surface before painting, consider scraping the rust off the nail heads and putting a rust-resistant primer on them.

Before staining an uneven-grained wood, especially a softwood, consider using an appropriate wood conditioner to help achieve a more even absorption. Bleaching a wood that has been grayed by weathering can improve it for staining or clear coating.

Sometimes minor dents and nicks on interior woods can be fixed by using a combination steam iron and damp cloth on them. Wood putty can be used to fill cracks and holes in wood surfaces you're painting; glazing or regular white putty doesn't stain well.

Open-grained woods such as oak, ash, chestnut, elm, hickory, and mahogany may need a wood paste filler if you want a smooth, nonporous look under a clear coating. These fillers come in different colors to match different woods and stains. *See also* **Refinishing, Prep work, Paneling,** and **Paint.**

Wood preservative is a clear, penetrating finish designed for outdoor use that fights moisture, mildew, rot, and decay. Use a clear wood preservative at package consistency for best results. Wood preservatives can be applied by spraying, rolling, brushing, and dipping. Remember wood preservatives work by penetration, so previous coats of varnish or paint must be removed before applying it. Some particular brands of wood preservatives claim they work just fine when applied over previously painted surfaces, but the more penetration the better. For color, some products combine a stain with a wood preservative. Formulations are improving all the time, but no product will preserve wood forever, so plan on repainting periodically. *See also* **Wood** and **Maintenance painting.**

Yellowing is a process that occurs when a white or off-white paint turns yellow. Very cheap paints will cause yellowing more readily than top-of-the-line paints. There are some paints that guarantee not to yellow for a specified length of time. Check the label.

Zinc dust is used in the making of many good metal primers. Zinc is corrosion- and rust-resistant.

About the Author

WILL CHARNOW has been a professional painter for seventeen years and a contractor for twelve. He has, as a result, extensive experience in residential, commercial, and industrial painting. Having learned many trade tips early on from employees of paint stores, he now returns the favor by lecturing to paint manufacturers and their field personnel on a recurring basis.

Mr. Charnow resides in Santa Barbara, California, his hometown.